INDUSTRIAL STRUCTURE IN THE NEW
INDUSTRIAL ECONOMICS

INDUSTRIAL STRUCTURE IN THE NEW INDUSTRIAL ECONOMICS

Giacomo Bonanno
and
Dario Brandolini

Clarendon Press · Oxford
1990

Oxford University Press, Walton Street, Oxford OX2 6DP

Oxford New York Toronto
Delhi Bombay Calcutta Madras Karachi
Petaling Jaya Singapore Hong Kong Tokyo
Nairobi Dar es Salaam Cape Town
Melbourne Auckland

and associated companies in
Berlin Ibadan

Oxford is a trade mark of Oxford University Press

Published in the United States
by Oxford University Press, New York

British Library Cataloguing in Publication Data
Bonanno, Ciacomo
Industrial structure in new industrial economics
1. Industries. Organisation structure
I. Title   II. Brandolini, Dario
338.7
ISBN 0–19–828645–7

Library of Congress Cataloging in Publication Data
Industrial structure in the new industrial economics / Giacomo Bonanno and
Dario Brandolini, editors.
p. cm.
Based on a series of lectures organized by the Associazione Borsiti
Luciana Jona.
1. Industrial organization (Economic theory)   I. Bonanno, Giacomo.
II. Brandolini Dario
HD2326.I518   1989   338.6—dc20   89–17362
ISBN 0–19–828645–7

Printed and bound in
Great Britain by Courier International Ltd,
Tiptree, Essex.

Preface

This volume is based on a series of lectures on the theme 'The New Industrial Economics', which took place at the Fondazione Luigi Einaudi of Turin in 1987 and the first half of 1988. The lectures were organized by the Associazione Borsisti Luciano Jona and made possible by the generous financial support of the Istituto Bancario San Paolo di Torino and the courteous hospitality of the Fondazione Einaudi.

The Associazione Borsisti Luciano Jona was created in 1982 and counts now more than two hundred members, all of whom have been recipients of 'Luciano Jona' scholarships, generously provided by the Istituto Bancario San Paolo in order to enable Italian graduates to pursue advanced research abroad—mainly in the United Kingdom and the United States—particularly in the field of economics. The aim of the Associazione is to create and maintain fruitful contacts between the Italian centres of economic debate and the foreign universities at which its members studied and in some cases are now teaching. Given the great success of the first lecture series, the Associazione now intends to organize a series every year and thereby cover a broad range of subjects within the field of economics. Industrial Organization was chosen as the first topic because of the unprecedented growth of the theoretical literature in the field. The need was felt for comprehensive and up-to-date surveys of the literature and indeed the same character will be maintained for future lecture series. The contributions in this volume provide a state-of-the-art account of important areas in Industrial Organization and the authors are among the most active contributors in the field.

G. B.
D. B.

The Associazione Borsisti Luciano Jona brings together economists to whom the San Paolo Bank of Turin has awarded scholarships to pursue post-graduate studies abroad. The bank has awarded scholarships since 1981 and at present the Associazione has around 200 members. After completing their studies abroad, some members have accepted job offers from foreign universities or institutions, others have taken up jobs in Italy. Consequently, the Associazione regroups economists holding interesting positions in institutions of various countries. The aims of the Associazione are twofold: to maintain and strengthen contacts among its members through the 'Luciano Jona Working Papers' on economic topics and, with the financial support of San Paolo Bank, to organize initiatives to increase exchanges between foreign universities and Italian centres of economic research.

Contents

1

Introduction

Giacomo Bonanno and Dario Brandolini

Industrial organization as a separate field of economic inquiry, with well-defined scope and boundaries, came into being in the late 1930s. The label 'industrial organization' and the initial impetus to develop the field are due to Edward S. Mason of Harvard University. The initial contributions to the field consisted of empirical studies, mainly detailed case studies of particular industries, with the main focus on pricing policy and, in particular, the policies of large industrial firms.

The seminal work of Joe S. Bain (1951, 1956), one of Mason's Ph.D. students, led to a shift in research interests in the 1960s from single-industry studies to inter-industry, cross-section analyses. Bain's complaint with previous work was that empirical research until then had made 'little definite progress in establishing an objective classification of markets, with subcategories which would contain industries with uniform and definitive types of competitive behaviour' (Bain 1948: 158). Until the late 1970s contributions to the industrial organization literature, which remained almost entirely empirical, were inspired by the theoretical tenet that 'the organization and structure of the market determine conduct and performance'. The traditional framework sought to explain the performance of the firm in terms of the firm's conduct in the market. The firm's conduct was in turn considered to be dependent on the organization and structure of the market, which was largely taken as exogenous. To quote Richard Caves, 'market structure is important because the structure determines the behaviour of firms in the industry and that behaviour in turn determines the quality of industries' performance' (Caves 1967: 16). This structure-conduct-performance paradigm inspired research in industrial organization until very recently and it is perhaps worth expanding on it a little.

In Bain's words,

market *structure* refers to the organizational characteristics of a market, and for practical purposes to those characteristics which determine the relations (*a*) of sellers in the market to each other, (*b*) of buyers in the market to each other, (*c*) of the sellers to the buyers, and (*d*) of sellers established in the market to potential new firms which might enter it (Bain 1968: 7).

Bain distinguishes four main aspects of market structure:

1. The *degree of seller concentration*—described by the number and the size distribution of sellers in the market.
2. The *degree of buyer concentration*—defined similarly.
3. The *degree of product differentiation* among the outputs of the various sellers in the market.
4. The *conditions of entry*—referring to the relative ease or difficulty with which new sellers may enter the market, as determined generally by the advantages which established sellers have over potential entrants (ibid.).

Each firm controls a number of decision variables such as methods and scale of production, advertising, research and development activities, prices, etc. The process of choosing between alternative levels of these decision variables is usually referred to as the behaviour, or *conduct*, of the firm.

Finally, the extent to which the levels of decision variables selected by a firm achieve various concepts of economic efficiency, including allocative, technical, and distributive efficiency, is referred to as *economic performance*.

The way in which the causal flow from structural features to firms' conduct and, therefore, to economic performance, was seen to operate is as follows:

The effect of any set of decision variables on the firm's revenues and costs will depend on the behaviour of buyers and other sellers. Buyers' behaviour depends on their objectives, usually taken to be the maximization of personal satisfaction, and on constraints such as income, tastes and information concerning available goods and services and terms of sale. Firms can influence buyer behaviour by altering some of these constraints and, therefore, the choice-set confronting the buyer. However, the effect of a particular firm's activities on its revenues depends also on the behaviour of other sellers, because this also influences the choices confronting buyers and, therefore, buyer behaviour . . . In deciding upon the level of its various decision variables, a firm's decision-makers will therefore treat the factors underlying the behaviour of buyers and other sellers as constraints, and the perceived nature of these constraints will influence the levels of decision variables selected by the firm's decision-makers. The structural features ⌊referred to above] influence the nature of some of the perceived constraints confronting firms' decision-makers, thereby in turn affecting the optimal level of decision variables and the resulting economic performance of the firm (Needham 1978: 2).

Market Structure

Market Concentration
Product Differentiation
Barriers to Entry
Vertical Integration
Cost Conditions
Scale Economies
Number of Buyers
Diversification

Conduct

Advertising
Research and Development
Pricing Strategy
Collusion
Production Policy

Performance

Technical Efficiency
Allocative Efficiency
Profitability
Technical Progress
Growth

Fig. 1.1 The Structure-Conduct-Performance Paradigm

The generality of the structure-conduct-performance paradigm (see Figure 1.1) caused attention to be focused on features which were common to different industries, rather than upon the idiosyncrasies of particular industries. For example, the number of firms in an industry was regarded as a prime determinant of the degree of co-operation among firms, which in turn would determine their levels of profit. Empirical correlations were sought between the degree of concentration of an industry and its profitability, and the relationship between the two variables was interpreted causally.

In the last ten years the economics of industrial organization has been undergoing major change and the structure-conduct-performance paradigm has been abandoned. New methods of analysis, mainly recent developments in the theory of non-co-operative games, have been employed and a substantial rethinking of the causes, nature, and effects of competitive behaviour has taken place. The new literature which has emerged has been mainly theoretical in character and has been referred to by many authors as 'The New Industrial Organization' (see e.g. Schmalensee 1982).

Perhaps the main feature of the new approach is that industrial structure is no longer taken to be the exogenous determinant of firms' conduct and performance, but an element which is itself in need of explanation. The basic assumption is that of non-co-operative behaviour by firms and the approach is to take nothing as given beyond the fundamental conditions of consumers' preferences and technology.

A second, important feature of the new approach is the recognition that firms—and economic agents in general—make sequential decisions over time and do so in a rational way, by taking into account the consequences of their actions on the subsequent evolution of industrial activity. Dynamic models have tended to replace static ones and new equilibrium concepts from game theory have been employed (mainly subgame-perfect, sequential, trembling-hand-perfect).

A third characterizing feature of the New Industrial Organization is the explicit modelling of differential and asymmetric information. It is recognized that, in general, buyers and sellers do not have perfect knowledge of the characteristics of their opponents, their preferences, their motivation, and their constraints. Situations of complete and incomplete information are treated differently and different equilibrium concepts are employed.

One of the implications of the new approach is that the aim of the structure-conduct-performance paradigm of finding a general theoretical framework capable of yielding simple generalizations and enabling one to extract the essential common features from different industries must be abandoned: it seems inevitable that we must develop a whole range of models from which one model specific to the market under study can be selected.

In what follows we shall mainly concentrate on various aspects of the New Industrial Organization pertaining to the problem of explaining or 'endogenizing' industrial structure and in the process provide a framework for considering the contributions in this book.

1.   Product Differentiation

Until very recently, the analysis of product differentiation was highly unsatisfactory and incomplete. Bain considered product differentiation as one of the main aspects of the structure of an industry and identified its sources as follows:

The sources of product differentiation within an industry encompass all considerations which may induce buyers to prefer one competing output to another. The most obvious ones are differences in quality or design among outputs . . . A second source of product differentiation is the ignorance of buyers regarding the essential characteristics and qualities of the goods they are purchasing . . . Third, buyer preferences for certain products are developed or shaped by the persuasive sales-promotion activities of sellers, and particularly by advertising . . . Finally, some product differentiation may result from differences in the locations of sellers of the same sort of good, which result in various buyers in the market being situated at different distances from different sellers (Bain 1968: 226–8).

In the spirit of the structure-conduct-performance paradigm, Bain then proceeds to list the effects of product differentiation on market conduct and performance: sellers are not bound to sell their products at a single common price, there will be incentives for sellers to undertake advertising and sales-promotional expenditures, sellers will tend to make adjustments in the design and quality of their products over time, etc. (ibid. 30, 228–35).

As the above quotation shows, the traditional approach failed to recognize the strategic incentives of firms to differentiate their products and to analyse the resulting effects on market structure. In the recent literature a distinction has emerged between *horizontal* product differentiation—a situation where, if prices are equal, different consumers will patronize different sellers—and *vertical* differentiation—where, when prices are the same, all consumers will choose the same product: the high-quality one (this terminology is from Lancaster 1979). For the case of horizontal differentiation, D'Aspremont, Gabszewicz, and Thisse (1979), elaborating on the original contribution of Hotelling (1929), showed that the degree of product differentiation may be the result of firms' incentive to reduce price competition (see also Economides 1986). Later, Gabszewicz and Thisse (1979, 1980) and Shaked and Sutton (1982) extended the result to the case of vertical differentiation (see also Bonanno 1986a). The general prediction which has emerged from this literature is that when competition is in prices, firms will never choose to produce a homogeneous product (provided that technology and consumers' tastes make differentiation possible). However, nothing can be said in general as to the *degree* of product differentiation which will emerge in equilibrium. On the other hand, this prediction does not extend to situations where firms compete not in prices but in output levels: in the case of vertical differentiation the incentives to differentiate may disappear and firms may decide to produce a homogeneous product (Bonanno 1986a).

Another interesting question which has been raised is whether firms' incentives to relax price competition through product differentiation will lead to an industry characterized by a large number of firms—each with a small share of the market—or to a concentrated structure. In a number of recent papers Shaked and Sutton (1983, 1987a, 1987b) have shown that the answer to this question varies according to the type of product differentiation (vertical versus horizontal) and depends in a subtle way on the interaction between consumer preferences and the technology of product improvement. The second chapter in this volume, 'Endogenous Sunk Costs and Industrial Structure', by John Sutton, provides an up-to-date account of some of the main issues in the area of product differentiation.

2.   Barriers to Entry

The 'condition of entry' is another aspect of industry structure which was emphasized in the structure-conduct-performance paradigm. In Bain's words,

The condition of entry into an industry denotes roughly the advantages in terms of cost or selling price which established firms have over potential entrant firms. It may be measured by the degree to which established firms can persistently elevate their prices above minimal average or competitive costs without making it attractive for new firms to enter (Bain 1968: 31).

Bain suggested the following categories into which industries could be classified:

1. *Easy entry*—that is, no barriers at all;
2. *Moderately difficult entry*—barriers to entry are appreciable but not high enough to permit established sellers to set a joint monolopy price without attracting entry;
3. *Blockaded entry*—barriers to entry are high enough that established sellers can set a joint monopoly price without attracting entry (ibid.).

As far as the source of such entry barriers, Bain thought that they could all be reduced to three main categories (ibid. 255):

1. Product differentiation advantages of established over potential entrant firms.
2. Absolute cost advantages of established over potential entrant firms.
3. Advantages of established over potential entrant firms due to economies of large-scale firms.

Thus, the source of entry barriers was seen to lie in the preferences of consumers or the characteristics of the technology, and the possibility that such structural elements might be 'artificially' manipulated by existing firms in order to erect a barrier to entry was not considered. On the other hand, the ease of entry was considered to have a direct effect on firms' conduct. To quote Bain again,

The condition of entry, or height of the barrier to entry to an industry, should in theory tend to influence its market conduct and performance in two ways. First, it places a long-run limit on selling price which established firms may choose not to exceed in order to forestall entry . . . Second, the decision of established firms to exceed the limit price will induce entry, increase industry output, and probably tend in the long run to keep that price from being exceeded (ibid. 31).

Theorists in industrial organization soon realized that the classical analysis of barriers to entry was deficient in two ways. First of all, the notion that potential entrants would base their decision to enter or not on the price chosen by the established firms, implied irrational behaviour on the part of the entrants: a rational entrant should realize that what matters from the point of view of the profitability of entry is the price which will prevail *after* entry and not the pre-entry price (cf. Friedman 1979). Moreover, there seems to be no necessary connection between the two. Secondly, there may be other ways in which established firms can, through their actions, discourage *rational* potential entrants from entering the industry.

A useful distinction was introduced by Salop (1979) between innocent and strategic barriers to entry. In choosing its policy, an existing firm might or might not take into account its effect on the expected profitability of entry for another firm. If the incumbent firm does not take the possibility of entry into account and nevertheless its policy has the effect of making entry unprofitable, then we say that an *innocent* barrier to entry has been erected (this corresponds to Bain's 'blockaded entry'). If, on the other hand, the incumbent firm takes an action which it would not take if it were protected from entry, and has the effect of deterring entry of other firms, then we say that a *strategic* barrier to entry has been erected. Strategic entry barriers are a clear example of how firms' conduct may affect industry structure and, therefore, of how the causal flow of the structure-conduct-performance paradigm might in fact be reversed.

When potential entrants are rational and there is complete information, the incumbent firm's actions can give rise to a strategic barrier to entry only if they satisfy two conditions: (i) they must have a lasting effect on demand and/or cost conditions, and (ii) they must represent an *irreversible commitment*. Thus, the cost of taking those actions must be *sunk costs*. In the last eight years a number of ways in which firms can erect strategic barriers to entry have been investigated, among which are the following:

(i)   investment in excess capacity (Dixit 1980);
(ii) investment in R. & D. (Gilbert and Newbery 1982, Brander and Spencer 1983);

(iii) advertising (Spence 1980, Cubbin 1981, Schmalensee 1983, Bonanno 1986*b*);

(iv) product proliferation (Schmalensee 1978, Bonanno 1987*a*);

(v) contracts with customers (Aghion and Bolton 1987).

While the recent literature on strategic entry deterrence has pointed out a number of possibilities which had been ignored in the past, it is now quite clear that no simple and general predictions have emerged. Predictions tend to depend in a crucial way on the hypotheses and structure of the particular model employed, both of which are often difficult—if not impossible—to test empirically.[1]

Related to the above literature is the theory of contestable markets, put forward by Baumol, Panzar and Willig (1982). A contestable market is one in which there are no impediments to entry: all firms—established and potential—have access to the same technology and hence face the same cost function. Furthermore, and most importantly—exit from a contestable market is absolutely costless, in the sense that there are no *sunk* (i.e. irrecoverable) costs of entry. Furthermore, it is assumed that existing firms are somewhat committed to their present prices. It follows that a contestable market is vulnerable to hit-and-run entry: 'Even a very transient opportunity need not be neglected by a potential entrant, for he can go in, and, before prices change, collect his gains and then depart without cost, should the climate grow hostile' (Baumol 1982: 4). At equilibrium in a contestable market the number and size of firms is always such that industry's output is produced at minimum total cost, profits are zero, and, when there are two or more firms in the market, price equals marginal cost. Baumol, Panzar and Willig, therefore, observe that competition has more to do with ease of entry and exit than with the presence of a large number of small firms (normally associated with the notion of perfect competition). The configuration of firms in a contestable

---

[1] It should also be noted that the central hypothesis of this literature, namely, that the economic agents involved (and the potential entrants in particular) are 'perfectly rational', is one, the justifiability of which, is an empirical question. Furthermore, the possibility that the incumbent's sunk cost is not observed or correctly assessed by the potential entrant, and/or that entry is probable rather than certain, affects the standard results in a non-negligible way (see Bonanno 1988). Finally, the concept of rationality itself has recently come under scrutiny in game theory (cf. Binmore 1987, Bonanno 1987*b*).

market is determined endogenously, and the existence of only a few firms can be perfectly consistent with strong competition.

The third chapter in this volume, 'The Role of Potential Competition in Industrial Organization', by Richard Gilbert, deals with these issues. The author's goal in this paper 'is to assemble some empirical evidence that can be brought to bear on the question of which theory, if any, is consistent with the available evidence.' Gilbert notes that his task is made difficult by the fact that 'little of the theory of entry prevention has been developed with the intention of providing empirically testable results.' The author identifies four alternative hypotheses:

(i)   contestable markets;
(ii) the Bain-Sylos-Modigliani model of limit pricing;
(iii) the dynamic limit-pricing model;
(iv) the Chicago School view, according to which profits are simply rents that accrue to superior technology;

and examines the support that empirical evidence (from simulation experiments and industry studies) provides for each of them. He then examines the literature on strategic entry deterrence. Not surprisingly, the conclusion is that the available empirical evidence does not yield clear-cut answers on the question of which theory better explains observed firm behaviour.

3.   Concentration and Collusion

In the classical approach the degree of concentration was considered to be one of the main structural features of an industry and therefore one of the main determinants of firms' conduct and performance. In Bain's words:

Why should market conduct and performance be expected to respond to variations in seller concentration among oligopolistic industries? To answer this, we must explore briefly the theoretical reasoning that establishes the causal linkage which runs from degree of seller concentration, through strength of mutually recognized interdependence, to market conduct and performance (Bain 1968: 118).

This line of reasoning is based on the recognition that each firm in an oligopolistic industry has two conflicting desires: (i) the desire to act co-operatively and choose an output which maximizes joint profits, and (ii) the desire to increase its own share of the market at the expense of rival sellers (ibid.). One of the predictions which Bain draws is the following:

The structure of an oligopolistic industry, and in particular its degree and pattern of seller concentration, may be expected to influence strongly the comparative force of the two motivations in determining market conduct and performance. Under one extreme set of structural conditions, more or less 'automatic' choice by all sellers of a joint profit-maximizing price and output policy, with no independent and antagonistic action, might be expected. These conditions are: (1) The sellers are few enough and all have large enough market shares to recognize mutual interdependence. (2) In addition, their proportion of total industry sales (shares of the market) at any common price are equal. (3) Their 'cost conditions' are identical—i.e., each has the same relationship of cost of production to output—so that they have an identical view of the level of the most profitable joint price. (4) Any price or output change by any seller will be immediately known by and draw an instantaneous response from his rivals, with the result that no independent move by any seller can gain him, either temporarily or permanently, any increase in his share of the market. If all of these structural conditions were fulfilled in an oligopoly, no seller therein could ever gain any advantage from independent, antagonistic action. The joint profit-maximizing motivation should be the only operative one (Bain 1968: 119).

The theoretical foundations for such claims were lacking and much work needed to be done in order to provide a coherent theory of non-co-operative collusion. In the past ten years a vast literature has emerged on this topic.

On the one hand, there is the literature on *repeated games* which has shown that even in the absence of explicit, enforceable agreements between firms, co-operative outcomes can indeed emerge if the strategic interaction is repeated over time (Friedman 1977, Abreu 1982, Fudenberg and Maskin 1986). For lasting, non-co-operative collusion to be possible in repeated games, a number of conditions need to be satisfied, in particular:

(i) the game must be repeated indefinitely;[2] and

---

[2] The view that rational co-operation in a Prisoners' Dilemma type of situation is not possible if the game is only repeated a finite number of times is almost unanimous, but its logical foundations can be questioned (see Bonanno 1987*b*). Some degree of co-operation in finitely repeated games where the constituent game

(ii) players must attach enough weight to the future in their calculations.[3]

On the other hand, there is a much smaller and relatively more recent literature which is reviewed by Jean Jaskold Gabszewicz in the fourth chapter in this volume, entitled 'The Stability of Collusive Agreements: Some Recent Theoretical Developments'. One of the questions considered in this paper is what happens in situations where a group of firms in an industry contemplate forming a cartel which will then act as a price leader. As Stigler noted, the problem here is that the outsiders of a cartel agreement will in general be better off than the insiders:

The major difficulty in forming a merger is that it is more profitable to be outside a merger than to be a participant. The outsider sells at the same price but at the much larger output at which marginal cost equals price. Hence the promoter of a merger is likely to receive much encouragement from each firm—almost every encouragement, in fact, except participation (Stigler 1950: 24).

Gabszewicz notes that a rational cartel member will not simply conclude that, since outsiders' profits are higher, it is in his interest to leave the cartel and join the competitive fringe: he will realize that his action will determine a switch to a new industry equilibrium and it is his profit at this new equilibrium which represents the relevant term of comparison. Similarly, a member of the fringe who contemplates joining the cartel will have to take into account how his action will affect the industry equilibrium. These observations lead Gabszewicz to define the notions of internal and external stability of a cartel and to investigate the conditions for the existence of stable cartels. The author also reviews the literature on a number of related topics: the profitability of horizontal mergers when competition is in output levels, the incentives to form syndicates which bind their members by preventing them from forming sub-coalitions, the possibility of situations of 'quasi-monopoly' arising when firms have capacity constraints.

admits several equilibria has also been shown to be possible (cf. Benoit and Krishna 1985).

[3] There are also other important factors, such as the possibility of detecting 'cheating' unambiguously (cf. Green and Porter 1984 and Abreu *et al.* 1986).

4. Vertical Structure

The classical approach dealt mainly with the *horizontal* aspect of industry structure, that is, with the interaction between firms which are at the same stage of the same production process. The study of the *vertical* aspect, that is, the relationship between firms which operate at different stages of the same productive process, was almost absent and dealt mainly with the technological advantages of vertical integration.

A large, and still growing, literature has emerged in the past ten years on the vertical aspects of industry structure. On the one hand, there is the transaction cost approach to vertical integration—and, more in general, to the problem of the internal organization of the firm—which was mainly pioneered by Oliver Williamson. In Williamson's words,

The factors that give rise to vertical integration are legion. Technology is widely believed to be one of them. The transaction cost approach does not deny that technology has a bearing but holds that, contrary to earlier traditions—e.g. Bain (1968: 381)—technology is rarely determinative. The main factor that is responsible for vertical integration from a transaction-cost point of view is asset specificity. Take this away, and autonomous contracting between successive production stages has good economizing properties in respect both of production cost and transaction cost. As asset specificity increases, however, the balance shifts in favour of vertical integration (Williamson 1986: 157).

On the other hand, there is the literature on vertical restraints, which are contractual agreements between manufacturers and retailers establishing a limit to what the retailer or manufacturer can do. The most common forms of vertical restraints are: resale price maintenance (fixing the consumer price or setting a floor/ceiling to it), franchise fees (a lump-sum transfer to be paid by one of the parties—normally the retailer—independent of the size of the transaction), exclusive territories (assigning a given geographical area to one retailer only), exclusive dealing (prohibiting the retailer from distributing goods from other manufacturers). The widespread use of various forms of vertical restraints in different industries makes a theoretical understanding of the phenomenon essential from the point of view of public policy and, in particular, of antitrust regulation. While, in general, vertical restraints enhance the efficiency of the vertical structure, and often provide a substitute for vertical integration, the overall welfare implications are more ambiguous. It is therefore important to develop a whole range of models which capture different incentives for the use of vertical restraints and enable us to distinguish between those cases in which vertical restraints benefit consumers, as well as the vertical structure, and those in which the vertical structure's gain is at the expense of other groups of agents.

The fifth chapter in this volume, 'Competition-Reducing Vertical Restraints', by Jean Tirole, provides a survey of the most recent contributions to this literature. Tirole deals mainly with papers which appeared in the last two years and were, therefore, not covered by a previous survey that he wrote in collaboration with Patrick Rey (Rey and Tirole 1986). The focus of Tirole's paper is on those vertical restraints whose purpose is to reduce competition between retailers (or, in general, agents). A number of new insights into this matter have been provided in the past two years.

5. Information and Uncertainty

The literature on the economics of uncertainty and information, stimulated by Akerlof's (1970) classic paper on consumer uncertainty about product quality, has been growing at a very fast rate. In recent years, one of the most active areas of research within this field has been the use of non-co-operative games of incomplete information to model industrial competition. In these models some firms (players) have *private information*—that is, information which is not shared by the other firms—concerning certain relevant parameters, such as cost and demand parameters. However, the probability distribution over what the particular private information of the various players could be is common knowledge. The existence of this type of private information can lead to complex strategic behaviour: bluffing, signalling, reputation building, etc. In his influential book *The Strategy of Conflict* (1960) Thomas Schelling defined a strategic move (such as a threat or a promise) as a move designed to influence the behaviour of others. One way in which a player can do this is by influencing the *beliefs* of his opponents. In situations of asymmetric information a less-informed firm will make inferences from the behaviour of a more-informed rival. Hence the latter has an incentive to engage in such activities as bluffing and signalling.

The use of models of asymmetric information has proved to be very effective in providing a theoretical foundation for phenomena such as limit pricing aimed at deterring entry. We noted above that, if there is complete and perfect information, a rational potential entrant's decision whether or not to enter a given market is independent of the pre-entry price set by the incumbent. If, however, the incumbent has private information concerning some objective parameters which have a direct effect on the profitability of entry (e.g. the incumbent's costs), then the pre-entry price can be used as an instrument to influence the potential entrant's beliefs concerning the value of these parameters. A rational potential entrant, however, will be aware of the incumbent's incentives and therefore his beliefs cannot be systematically biased by the signalling behaviour. At equilibrium the entrant has correct conjectures regarding the incumbent's actions (as a function of the incumbent's information) and accounts for these in making inferences about the parameters (Milgrom and Roberts 1982).

Besides limit pricing, a number of phenomena have been rationalized by means of game-theoretic models of incomplete information: image advertising, introductory sales, etc. (for a fairly comprehensive survey see Milgrom and Roberts 1987).

Another phenomenon which is hard to explain if the players concerned have complete and perfect information as to the value of all the relevant parameters, is *predatory pricing*. In fact, a number of authors (for example, McGee (1980)) have claimed that predatory pricing cannot be part of a deliberate, rational competitive strategy and that, therefore, apparent instances of it are likely to be misinterpretations; furthermore, any form of legislation on predatory pricing would only have the undesirable effect of protecting inefficient firms from the discipline of competition. The sixth chapter in this volume, 'New Theories of Predatory Pricing', by Paul Milgrom and John Roberts, contains a comprehensive and up-to-date survey of the literature on this topic. The authors define predatory pricing as 'the temporary charging of particularly low prices in order to improve long-run profitability by inducing exit, deterring entry, or "disciplining" rivals into accepting relatively small market shares.' The first section examines the possibility of predatory pricing in situations where there is no asymmetric information, but there are either inter-temporal linkages in demand or asymmetries in firms' ability to sustain temporary losses. The second section is concerned with models of asymmetric information of the type discussed above. Throughout the chapter Milgrom and Roberts discuss the policy implications which can be drawn from the various models and provide a critical examination of the legislation and case law on the matter of predatory pricing.

6.   Recent Empirical Studies

We noted at the beginning, and it should have become apparent from the above discussion, that non-co-operative game theory has played a prominent role in the development of the New Industrial Organization literature. The advantages associated with the use of game theory are widely recognized:

Game theory has had a deep impact on the theory of industrial organization, in a similar (but less controversial) way as the rational expectations revolution in macroeconomics. The reason it has been embraced by a majority of researchers in the field is that it imposes some discipline on theoretical thinking. It forces economists to clearly specify the strategic variables, their timing, and the information structure faced by firms. As is often the case in economics, the researcher learns as much from constructing the model (the 'extensive form') as from solving it because in constructing the model one is led to examine its realism. (Is the timing of entry plausible? Which variables are costly to change in the short-run? Can firms observe their rivals' prices, capacities, or technologies in the industry under consideration? etc.) (Fudenberg and Tirole 1987: 176).

Some authors, however, have recently become more and more suspicious about the usefulness of the game-theoretic approach to industrial organization. In the opening pages of his contribution to this volume—'Empirical Studies of Rivalrous Behaviour'—Richard Schmalensee observes that:

Unfortunately . . . the general impression that has emerged from a decade's extensive use of the game-theoretic approach is 'Anything can happen!' The diversity and growth of the theoretical literature provides a good deal of support for the conjecture that almost any remotely plausible pattern of conduct—anything that has ever been alleged with a straight face in an antitrust case, say—can appear in equilibrium in an apparently plausible game-theoretic model. Policy implications are in some sense even more varied, since efficient policy in many models depends on details of parameter values and functional forms.

Schmalensee's view that 'game-theoretic modelling has taught us a great deal about what *might* happen in a variety of situations, but relatively little about what *must* happen conditional on observables,' leads him to conclude that 'empirical research is absolutely critical to progress in the field of industrial organization.'

As Bresnahan and Schmalensee (1987: 373) observe, 'At the start of the 1980s relatively little exciting empirical work was being done in industrial organization: industry-level cross-section work was suspect, and case studies were no more attractive than they had been a decade earlier. The main action was on the theoretical side.' The 1980s, however, have witnessed a rebirth of research activity on the empirical side of industrial economics, leading the two above-mentioned authors to speak of an 'Empirical Renaissance in industrial economics' (ibid.).

The empirical research in this field has been developing along two different directions: (i) laboratory experiments, and (ii) studies of actual behaviour in real markets. Schmalensee's paper in this volume provides a survey of the latter.[4] The author first reviews the classical empirical industrial organization literature, which—as we noted at the beginning—developed along two different directions: the industry case studies (mainly during the period between the late 1930s and the early 1960s) and the cross-section profitability studies (during the 1960s and 1970s). Schmalensee also discusses a number of measurement and identification problems which undermined the validity of the classical empirical studies. In sections 4 and 5 of his paper, Schmalensee gives a comprehensive review of recent econometric intra-industry and inter-industry studies, respectively. The availability of new econometric techniques has made it possible partly to correct the measurement errors which plagued earlier empirical studies and to exploit more fully the information contained in the available data. Schmalensee concludes on a rather negative note:

It is important to note that virtually all of the persuasive empirical studies discussed here share one important feature: they employ carefully constructed data sets. Because few real data sets confess their secrets

---

[4] A comprehensive survey of the recent literature on experimental economics can be found in Plott 1988.

easily, advances in modelling techniques and econometric methods are important. But the main lesson that seems to emerge from recent developments in empirical research in industrial organization is that the quality of the results obtained depends critically on the quality of the data employed . . . This is in some respects a discouraging conclusion. Economists, unlike historians or anthropologists, are formally trained only in the analysis of data sets, not in their construction. The economics profession does not much reward the tedious labour necessary to construct sound and interesting data sets . . . Thus, progress in industrial organization may depend critically on the extent to which the construction of informative data sets is supported by government agencies and other sources of research financing.

References

Abreu, D. (1982), *Repeated Games with Discounting: A General Theory and an Application to Oligopoly*, Ph.D. thesis, Princeton University.

—— Pearce, D. and Stacchetti, E. (1986), 'Optimal Cartel Equilibria with Imperfect Monitoring', *Journal of Economic Theory*, 39: 251–69.

Aghion, P. and Bolton, P. (1987), 'Contracts as a Barrier to Entry', *American Economic Review*, 77: 388–401.

Akerlof, G. A. (1970), 'The Market for "lemons": Quality, Uncertainty and the Market Mechanism', *Quarterly Journal of Economics*, 84: 488–500.

Bain, J. S. (1948), 'Price and Production Policies', in H. S. Hellis (ed.), *A Survey of Contemporary Economics*, Irwin, Homewood, Ill.

—— (1951), 'Relation of Profit Rate to Industry Concentration: American Manufacturing, 1936–40', *Quarterly Journal of Economics*, 65: 293–324.

—— (1956), *Barriers to New Competition*, Harvard University Press, Cambridge, Mass.

—— (1968), *Industrial Organization*, 2nd edn., John Wiley and Sons, New York.

Baumol, W. (1982), 'Contestable Markets: An Uprising in the Theory of Industry Structure', *American Economic Review*, 72: 1–15.

—— Panzar, J. and Willig, R. D. (1982), *Contestable Markets and the Theory of Industry Structure*, Harcourt Brace Jovanovich, New York.

Benoit, J.-P. and Krishna, V. (1985), Finitely Repeated Games, *Econometrica*, 53: 905–22.

Binmore, K. (1987), 'Modelling Rational Players: Part I', *Economics and Philosophy*, 3: 179–214.

Bonanno, G. (1986a), 'Vertical Differentiation with Cournot Competition', *Economic Notes*, 15: 68–91.

—— (1986b), 'Advertising, Perceived Quality and Strategic Entry Deterrence and Accommodation', *Metroeconomica*, 38: 257–80.

—— (1987a), 'Location Choice, Product Proliferation and Entry Deterrence', *Review of Economic Studies*, 54: 37–45.

—— (1987b), 'The Logic of Rational Play in Sequential Games', mimeo., University of California, Davis.

—— (1988), 'Entry Deterrence with Uncertain Entry and Uncertain Observability of Commitment', *International Journal of Industrial Organization*, 6: 351–62.

Brander, J. and Spencer, B. (1983), 'Strategic Commitment with R & D: The Symmetric Case', *Bell Journal of Economics*, 14: 225–35.

Bresnahan, T. F. and Schmalensee R. (1987), 'The Empirical Renaissance in Industrial Economics: An Overview', *Journal of Industrial Economics*, 35: 371–8.

Caves, R. E. (1967), *American Industry: Structure, Conduct, and Performance*, 2nd edn., Prentice-Hall, Englewood Cliffs, NJ.

Cubbin, J. (1981), 'Advertising and the Theory of Entry Barriers', *Economica*, 48: 289–98.

D'Aspremont, C., Gabszewicz, J. J., and Thisse, J.-F. (1979), 'On Hotelling's Stability in Competition', *Econometrica*, 47: 1145–50.

Dixit, A. (1980), 'The Role of Investment in Entry Deterrence', *Economic Journal*, 90: 95–106.

Economides, N. (1986), 'Minimal and Maximal Product Differentiation in Hotelling's Model', *Economics Letters*, 11: 19–23.

Friedman, J. (1977), *Oligopoly and the Theory of Games*, North-Holland, Amsterdam.

—— (1979), 'On Entry Preventing Behaviour and Limit Price Models of Entry', in S. J. Brams, A. Schotter, and G. Schwoediauer (eds.), *Applied Game Theory*, Physica-Verlag, Wuerzburg, 236–53.

Fudenberg, D. and Maskin, E. (1986), 'The Folk Theorem in Repeated Games with Discounting and with Incomplete Information', *Econometrica*, 54: 533–54.

—— and Tirole, J. (1987), 'Understanding Rent Dissipation: On the Use of Game Theory in Industrial Organization', *American Economic Review, Papers and Proceedings*, 77: 176–83.

Gabszewicz, J. J. and Thisse, J.-F. (1979), 'Price Competition, Quality and Income Disparities', *Journal of Economic Theory*, 20: 340–59.

—— (1980), 'Entry (and Exit) in a Differentiated Industry', *Journal of Economic Theory*, 22: 327–38.

Gilbert, R. and Newbery, D. (1982), 'Preemptive Patenting and the Persistence of Monopoly', *American Economic Review*, 72: 514–26.

Green, E. and Porter, R. (1984), 'Non-Cooperative Collusion under Imperfect Price Information', *Econometrica*, 52: 87–100.

Hotelling, H. (1929), 'Stability in Competition', *Economic Journal*, 39: 41–57.

Lancaster, K. (1979), *Variety, Equity and Efficiency*, Basil Blackwell, Oxford.

McGee, J. (1980), 'Predatory Pricing Revisited', *Journal of Law and Economics*, 23: 289–330.

Milgrom, P. and Roberts, J. (1982), 'Limit Pricing and Entry under Incomplete Information: An Equilibrium Analysis', *Econometrica*, 50: 443–59.

—— (1987), 'Informational Asymmetries, Strategic Behaviour, and Industrial Organization', *American Economic Review, Papers and Proceedings*, 77: 184–93.

Needham, D. (1978), *The Economics of Industrial Structure, Conduct and Performance*, St Martin's Press, New York.

Plott, C. R. (1988), 'An Updated Review of Industrial Organization Applications of Experimental Methods', in R. Schmalensee and R. D. Willig (eds.), *Handbook of Industrial Organization*, North-Holland, Amsterdam.

Rey, P. and Tirole, J. (1986), 'Vertical Restraints from a Principal–Agent Viewpoint', in L. Pellegrini and S. Reddy (eds.), *Marketing Channels: Relationship and Performance*, Lexington Books, Lexington, Mass.

Salop, S. (1979), 'Strategic Entry Deterrence', *American Economic Review, Papers and Proceedings*, 69: 335–8.

Schelling, T. (1960), *The Strategy of Conflict*, Harvard University Press, Cambridge, Mass.

Schmalensee, R. (1978), 'Entry Deterrence in the Ready-to-Eat Breakfast Cereal Industry', *Bell Journal of Economics*, 9: 305–27.

—— (1982), 'The New Industrial Organization and the Economic Analysis of Modern Markets', in W. Hildenbrand (ed.), *Advances in Economic Theory*, Cambridge University Press, Cambridge, 253–85.

—— (1983), 'Advertising and Entry Deterrence: An Exploratory Model', *Journal of Political Economy*, 91: 636–53.

Shaked, A. and Sutton, J. (1982), 'Relaxing Price Competition Through Product Differentiation', *Review of Economic Studies*, 49: 3–13.

—— (1983), 'Natural Oligopolies', *Econometrica*, 51: 1469–84.

—— (1987a), 'Product Differentiation and Industrial Structure', *Journal of Industrial Economics*, 36: 131–46.

—— (1987b), 'Multiproduct Firms and Market Structure', ST/ICERD Working Paper No. 154, London School of Economics.

Spence, A. M. (1980), 'Notes on Advertising, Economies of Scale, and Entry Barriers', *Quarterly Journal of Economics*, 95: 493–508.

Stigler, G. J. (1950), 'Monopoly and Oligopoly by Merger', *American Economic Review, Papers and Proceedings*, 40: 23–34.

Vickers, J. (1985), 'Strategic Competition Among the Few: Some Recent Developments in the Economics of Industry', *Oxford Review of Economic Policy*, 1: 39–62.

Williamson, O. (1986), 'Vertical Integration and Related Variations on a Transaction-Cost Economics Theme', in J. Stiglitz and F. Matthewson (eds.), *New Developments in the Analysis of Market Structure*, Macmillan, London.

2

Endogenous Sunk Costs and Industrial Structure

John Sutton

Discussions of the determinants of industrial structure have traditionally emphasized the role of three elements: the degree of scale economies present, the level of advertising expenditures, and the intensity of R & D activities.

The present chapter is concerned with unravelling some relations between these variables, and equilibrium structure. The central distinction made in the paper is between the manner of handling scale economies, on the one hand, and advertising and R & D on the other.

With regard to scale economies, the view taken here is that these may best be treated by introducing the notion of a 'set-up cost' identified with the cost of acquiring a single plant of minimum-efficient scale. This cost is a *sunk cost* and its size is *exogenously given*.

The first part of the paper is concerned with the question of how such costs should be analysed. We look at the role of these costs in a simple '2-stage game': firms decide at stage 1 whether or not to enter the industry, thereby incurring this sunk cost. At stage 2 those firms who have entered compete in price.

The central theme of this part of the chapter is that equilibrium structure depends on the interplay between the level of sunk cost incurred, and the intensity of price competition in the post-entry situation.

This leads us to the question of whether some systematic relationship should be expected between the degree of scale economies and equilibrium structure: an idea implicit in most of the traditional literature. We conclude from our discussion that this relationship turns out to be rather complex and problematic. Under carefully defined circumstances, however, a proposition can be developed which captures the traditional notion that industrial structure may be expected to become more and more fragmented as the ratio between set-up costs and the size of the market declines. So, as market size increases, other things being equal, we may converge to a 'fragmented' structure.

This proposition provides a point of departure for the second half of the chapter. Here, we are concerned with analysing the roles of advertising and R & D; we treat both of these as examples of what we term 'endogenous sunk costs'. These cost elements are both fixed, in the sense that they do not vary with the volume of output; and are sunk, in the sense of being irrecoverable.[1] The idea here is as follows: by increasing the level of these costs over the 'long run', in developing and advertising its products, the firm can increase consumers' 'willingness to pay' for its products relative to rivals' offerings. In those markets where such increases in *fixed* costs (as opposed to *variable* costs), are effective in raising consumers' 'willingness to pay', there is an in-built tendency in favour of a competitive escalation of expenditures on R & D and advertising. The most fundamental consequence of this is that increases in the size of the market do *not* imply a more fragmented structure. On the contrary, as market size increases, the returns from a given increase in fixed outlays rise, and so we tend to see an increased level of equilibrium outlays rather than a tendency towards fragmentation.

In the final section we explore some aspects of market structure which are likely to appear under these circumstances.

This chapter draws heavily on Shaked and Sutton 1987*a*, where the central results described below are established. The present contribution offers an informal introduction to the ideas set out in that article and elaborates on some aspects of the approach developed there.

1. The Role of Set-Up Costs

In the present section we set aside all considerations relative to advertising and R & D, and look at the role played by set-up costs in isolation. The natural way to begin is by looking at the

---

[1] In general, of course, fixed costs are not necessarily sunk costs. Moreover, on the basis of the definition of fixed cost used by Baumol and Willig (1981), sunk costs need not be fixed costs. It may be worth noting, however, that this definition is specific to the 'homogeneous product' case.

determination of structure in a 'homogeneous-goods' industry in which all firms offer an identical product. We may identify the 'set-up cost' incurred by firms on entering such an industry—at least as a first approximation—with the cost of acquiring a single plant of minimum-efficient scale, net of any 'resale value' which such a plant might have.

This irrecoverable element of fixed cost which must be incurred on entering the industry constitutes a 'sunk cost'; and so its level plays no role in determining the firm's day-to-day pricing policy subsequent to entry. This idea is neatly captured using the simple device of a '2-stage' game, as follows. We represent the firm's decision as taking place in two steps: at 'stage 1' each of a number of 'potential entrants' decides whether or not to enter. Then, at 'stage 2', those firms who have entered set their respective prices.

The 2-stage game device also serves to capture in a relatively simple manner the traditional distinction between 'long-run' and 'short-run' decisions. Those variables labelled 'long run', which are chosen at stage 1 of the game, are treated as fixed parameters when analysing equilibrium 'in the short run', as depicted in stage 2 of the game.

This way of representing the set-up costs associated with entry has an immediate implication which is of interest in what follows: prices set at stage 2 of the game depend on the set-up costs only *indirectly*, i.e. only by way of their influence on the entry decisions of firms in the first stage of the game. And so 'mistakes' involving excessive entry may lead to losses as prices set in the second stage may not suffice to cover the set-up costs incurred in entering the industry.

The entry decisions of firms in this set-up will depend on the *interplay* between the level of set-up cost incurred at stage 1, and the intensity of price competition which firms face at stage 2. The tougher the degree of price competition at stage 2, the lower will post-entry profits be, and the fewer the number of firms choosing to enter. Thus, equilibrium structure reflects a tension between the level of set-up costs which must be recovered in order to justify entry *ex post* and the intensity of price competition following entry: more entrants mean lower prices, but the lower the prices (for any given number of entrants), the less attractive will entry be.

It is now time to make these ideas more precise. We begin with a very elementary example, whose details are perhaps worth setting out in full, as it provides a useful point of departure for our later discussion.

Nash Equilibrium in Entry Decisions	Nash Equilibrium in Prices
Firms entering the industry incur a sunk cost	Firms compete in price. The outcome reflects the number of firms who have entered at Stage 1
Stage 1 Long-run Decisions	Stage 2 Short-run Decisions

Fig. 2.1 The '2-Stage Game' Formulation

A Model

Consider the 2-stage game illustrated in Figure 2.1. A firm's *strategy* in this game takes one of two forms: *either* 'don't enter', or else 'enter, and set price at stage 2 as a function of the number of firms who have entered at stage 1.' The firm's *pay-off* is either zero (if it chooses not to enter), or else it equals the profit earned at stage 2 less the sunk cost incurred at stage 1 (which we denote as ϵ, and which we assume to be strictly positive). Stage 2 profits are given as follows: total sales are given by the level of industry demand $q(p)$, and are shared equally among those firms who set the lowest price offered on the market. Suppose k firms set the equal lowest price $\underline{p}$. All those firms who have entered at stage 1 are assumed to produce under conditions of constant marginal cost c (unit variable cost) thereafter. Hence, a firm setting price p in period 2 earns profit $(p - c) q(p)/k$, if $p = \underline{p}$, and zero otherwise. To ensure viability we assume that the profits earned by a monopolist in this market exceed the set-up cost ϵ.

To analyse this game we begin by describing the equilibrium which results in the stage 2 subgame for each possible number of entrant firms. Our description above of firms' *strategies* implies we are looking for a Nash equilibrium in prices ('Bertrand equilibrium'), i.e. a set of prices such that, given the prices chosen by its rivals, each firm is setting an optimal price.

By the familiar Bertrand 'undercutting' argument, it is easy to see that if two or more firms enter, then price coincides with marginal cost and period 2 profits are zero.[2] If only one firm enters, then it sets the monopoly price at stage 2.

We now consider the entry decisions made at stage 1. We again look for a Nash equilibrium, i.e. a set of entry decisions such that, given its rivals' choices regarding entry, each firm is making an optimal decision. In other words we look for a (subgame) perfect equilibrium in the 2-stage game.

A moment's reflection makes the following result obvious:

Proposition 0: For any $\epsilon > 0$, the only outcome supported as a perfect equilibrium is one in which exactly one firm enters and sets the monopoly price.

To see this, note that, given a decision by one firm to enter, the optimal reply for any rival is 'don't enter'; for entering yields a net payoff of $(-\epsilon)$.

One striking feature of the preceding example is that this equilibrium outcome holds good for *any* positive value of set-up cost, up to the level of monopoly profit (beyond which the market is not 'viable').

Thus, if price competition is sufficiently intense, even a small level of set-up cost may suffice to deter entry.

It is interesting to ask what happens in the special case where ϵ is exactly zero ('no sunk costs'). In this case it is easy to show that many equilibria appear. Among them is the equilibrium already described (to see this, note that a potential entrant is *indifferent* between entering and not entering). Other equilibria involve two or more firms entering, and setting price equal to marginal cost. This latter equilibrium is analogous to those 'competitive' outcomes studied in the literature on 'contestable markets': it is worth noting the 'knife-edge' nature of this solution, which disappears once any level of sunk cost, however small, is present. It may be worth noting also that it is precisely at this point that the present analysis parts company with the 'contestability' approach: what is fundamental

---

[2] At equilibrium, at least two firms must be setting an equal lowest price $p = c$; and all firms with $p > \underline{p}$ will have zero sales. For otherwise at least one firm is not using an optimal reply to its rivals' prices. To see this, note that if $p < c$, the lowest-price firm(s) can raise its profit (to zero) by setting $p = c$; if $\underline{p} > c$, then any (equal) highest-price firm can raise its profits by slightly undercutting $\underline{p}$; while if only one firm is setting $\underline{p} = c$, then that firm can raise its profits by increasing its price.

to our present argument is that sunk costs are, in practice, almost always incurred in connection with long-run decisions on entry, advertising, and R & D and that the presence of such sunk costs plays a primary role in the determination of market structure.

A number of the arguments set out in the preceding section as to the *interplay* between set-up costs and the intensity of price competition in the market can easily be developed by means of routine extensions of the model just described. For example, we can replace Bertrand competition by Cournot competition[3] in the final stage of the game, so that equilibrium prices lie above marginal cost by some gap which falls as the number of entrants rises. This 'relaxation' in the intensity of price competition will lead to a larger number of entrants for any given level of set-up cost (below the 'duopoly profit' level).

The use of the 'Cournot' formulation also permits an illustration of the idea which we will take up in the next section: for a given 'form' of price competition[4]—here Cournot competition—we obtain an equilibrium outcome in which the number of entrants to the market increases steadily as the level of set-up cost ϵ falls from the level of monopoly profits (at which we have one entrant) to zero (in which limit the number of entrants becomes arbitrarily large, and price approaches marginal cost).

Extensions

The 'Cournot' version of the model just discussed constitutes the most elementary form of 'limit theorem' according to which increases in the size of the economy relative to the level of set-up costs lead to a more fragmented structure.

The theme of the present chapter concerns one of a number of important reasons why this kind of relationship may fail to hold good.

Three such reasons appear to be of some practical relevance.[5]

[3] i.e. a *strategy* is (re)defined as being: Either 'don't enter', *or* 'enter and set a level of output in stage 2 as a function of the number of firms who have entered at stage 1.'

[4] Simple though the device of 'assuming Cournot competition' is, it does conceal a fundamental issue—it is by no means clear in general what meaning can be attached to 'keeping the intensity of price competition constant', as the number of firms, and so equilibrium price, changes.

[5] A fourth hinges on the possibility that entry might *raise* unit margins, other things being equal. This rests on rather contrived assumptions, however, and its empirical relevance may be very limited (Sutton 1989*a*).

The first of these we have already seen: the 'limit theorem' idea rests on the notion that unit margins decline steadily as the number of firms increases. In the 'Bertrand' version of the above model, the entry of even two firms reduces margins to zero, thus precluding the recovery of sunk costs.[6]

Secondly, the idea embodied in the 'limit theorem' also rests on the notion that the sunk costs are *exogenously given*; in the next section we explore what happens if *endogenous* sunk costs are present.

There is, however, a third way in which the 'limit-theorem' idea must be qualified. This arises once we move beyond the homogeneous-product setting explored above, to one in which products are differentiated by location or by some other 'horizontal' attribute. (A set of products is said to be differentiated horizontally if, when all products are offered at the same price, each enjoys a positive market share. Such models are analogous to locational models, in which each firm's product is preferred, prices being equal, by consumers in its own 'locality'. The complementary case of 'vertical differentiation' is examined in the next section.)

Equilibria in models of horizontal product differentiation have been explored to some degree in the recent literature, some notable contributions being Schmalensee 1978, Lane 1980, and Bonanno 1987. A full discussion of their properties lies outside our present scope; the interested reader is referred to Shaked and Sutton 1987*a* for a characterization of equilibria.

The point relevant to our present discussion is that in this context multiple equilibria are endemic. Depending on the nature of demand (and cost) conditions, the models may permit—for a given level of set-up cost and market size—both 'fragmented' equilibria in which a large number of firms each offer one product, or 'concentrated' equilibria in which a small number of firms each offer several products. In developing 'limit theorems', it is often assumed that each firm can produce only a single variety; and this is the route which we follow in the next section. It should be emphasized, however, that the resulting relationship is best thought of either as representing merely a lower bound to the level of

---

[6] This case might at first glance appear to be too special a case to be of much practical interest; but it seems in fact to offer a natural point of departure in analysing a number of industries in which perfectly homogeneous goods are produced subject to substantial set-up costs and where a strong tendency towards collusive arrangements has typically been observed (Sutton (1989c.)).

concentration attainable for given levels of set-up costs and economy size, or as pertaining only to those (rather special) markets in which firms typically offer only a single variety (sell at a single location).

A 'Limit Theorem'

We now set out a limit theorem which characterizes equilibria in a class of models of 'horizontal product differentiation'.

We assume the '2-stage game' formulation developed earlier, with one difference. Here, the profit functions of firms in the final stage in which we seek a Nash equilibrium in prices (Bertrand equilibrium) are given by the following underlying specification of demand:

- Consumers are distributed along some closed interval according to a continuous density which is strictly positive everywhere; the area under this density function equals the population of consumers, S.

- Each consumer buys exactly one unit from some one firm. The firm chosen is that for which the consumer's utility

$$U^* - p - H(|h - \alpha|)$$

is maximized. Here, U^* is a constant, p denotes price, α is the consumer's location on the interval, h is the position of the product chosen, and $H(.)$ is a strictly increasing convex function.

We assume further that:

- Each firm ('potential entrant') can enter at stage 1 at any location h, at a sunk cost $\epsilon > 0$.

It is well known that stringent conditions may be required in order to ensure the existence of equilibrium in this set-up (see the comments and references in Shaked and Sutton 1987a). Here we confine ourselves merely to a characterization result, which depends only on the relatively mild assumptions stated above. Under these assumptions, the following result holds (for a proof, see Shaked and Sutton 1987a):

Proposition 1: For every $\epsilon > 0$ there exists an economy size (population) S^* such that in every equilibrium in a market of size $S > S^*$ each firm has a market share less than ϵ.

The intuition behind this result is straightforward: given any number of firms in the market, successive replications of the population of consumers raise the level of profits attainable by any given set of firms. So, as population increases, the maximal space between adjacent firms becomes arbitrarily small, as the profitability of 'filling a gap' between any pair of occupied locations rises. This in turn can be shown to imply that the maximal market share of any firm also becomes arbitrarily small.

2.   Endogenous Sunk Costs

Advertising expenditures devoted to building up the 'image' of a product, and R & D expenditures aimed at enhancing the 'perceived quality' of a product, have a fundamental feature in common: in each case an increase in fixed costs is undertaken by a firm as part of its long-term strategy with a view to enhancing consumers' willingness to pay for its product.

It is this feature of advertising and R & D which forms our starting-point here. These fixed outlays, like those considered above, can be treated as 'sunk costs'; the essential difference which enters here is that their level is determined endogenously as part of the underlying market equilibrium.

The way in which we model these expenditures derives from the literature on 'vertical product differentiation'. Products may differ in various attributes; some attributes (like colour, design, etc.) are best thought of as being 'horizontal' or 'location-like' in the sense that consumers differ in the direction of their preferences in respect of that attribute (some preferring one colour, and others a different colour). In contrast, a 'vertical' or 'quality-like' attribute is one on which all consumers agree ('more is better'). Much 'image advertising' as well as much R & D expenditure is geared towards enhancing the product's attractiveness for all consumers, and so we may think of it as involving the expenditure of fixed costs aimed at raising the vertical attribute (this can be measured by consumers' willingness to pay, once allowance is made for the fact that consumers differ in their willingness to pay. Thus, in the literature it is standard to introduce some (artificial) index or measure of the 'quality' attribute (and to use this in setting up consumers' utility functions).

Now, the enhancement of willingness to pay could in general involve an expenditure of both *fixed* and *variable* costs (while the former includes R & D and advertising outlays, the latter would include enhanced expenditure on labour or raw materials).

The central idea of the present section runs as follows: when the burden of 'quality improvement' falls primarily on *fixed* costs (as opposed to variable costs), then there is a strong tendency for the industry to assume a concentrated structure.

Various 'precise' formulations of this notion are possible (Shaked and Sutton 1983, Sutton 1986). Here we turn to the weakest and most general formulation, which runs in terms of a negation of the 'limit-theorem' idea set out above. In the present context, this kind of convergence to a fragmented structure in large economies turns out to be impossible. This result, moreover, turns out to be extremely robust to changes in the underlying model, as noted below.

A Model

The model used here is an extension of the 'horizontal' product differentiation model used in characterizing the 'fragmentation' property in section 1 above. Each consumer buys exactly one unit (or none) of one of a number of products on offer. Each product is characterized by two attributes: h measures a 'location-like' or 'horizontal' attribute, as before. We extend the earlier model by introducing a 'quality index' u, which measures the level of a vertical attribute. A consumer is characterized by his income Y (which determines his willingness to pay for a given quality improvement, or his 'sensitivity to quality'), and a number α, which represents his most preferred value of the 'horizontal' attribute.

A consumer's utility score on purchasing a unit of product (u,h) at price p is denoted by $U(u,d,y)$. Here d represents the distance $|h - \alpha|$ between the product's horizontal attribute and his most preferred value of that attribute; while y denotes $(Y - p)$, the income left to him following his purchase, which is spent on 'outside goods'.

We assume (trivially) that $U_u > 0$ and that $U_d < 0$. We also assume that $U_{uy} > 0$, i.e. richer consumers are willing to pay more for a given quality increment (this last assumption can in fact be relaxed—it merely serves to simplify matters).

We now turn to the specification of costs; it is here that we introduce the key assumption of the model. As we noted above, the central idea is that we are concerned with the case in which the main burden of 'quality' improvement falls on fixed costs rather than on variable costs. We model the cost structure by supposing that a firm offering a single product with attributes (u,h) incurs a fixed cost $F(u)$; we treat this expenditure as a sunk cost, incurred in stage 1 of the game.

In stage 2 of the game we model price competition as a Nash equilibrium in prices as before. Each firm is assumed to produce under conditions of constant marginal cost; but this level of marginal cost (or 'unit-variable cost') is allowed to depend on quality and is labelled $c(u)$.

To pin down the notion that the main burden of quality improvement falls on the fixed-cost component $F(u)$, there are two ways in which we can proceed. On the one hand, we can simply introduce a suitable set of assumptions on technology and tastes as follows:

First, we impose some mild 'technical' restrictions:

• U_u is bounded away from zero, and U_y and $|U_d|$ are bounded above.

Secondly, we introduce the key notion that quality improvement should not fall too heavily on *variable* costs, $c(u)$:

• $c(u)$ is bounded above by some income level which is less than the maximum value of consumer income, $\bar{Y}$.

This pair of assumptions deserves two comments. First, they are unnecessarily strong. Secondly, they are couched in terms of the utility indicator $U(u,d,y)$; in fact the introduction of such a function is merely a convenience. All that matters is the underlying mapping from firms' costs to consumers' willingness to pay—but the simplest way to represent that underlying mapping is by introducing a quality label u and a utility indicator $U(u,d,y)$.

For these reasons it is attractive to replace the preceding pair of assumptions with the following statement, which can be shown to follow from them.

A1: There exists some strictly positive triple (μ, p, δ), such that, if each firm offers a good with $u \leqslant \bar{u}$, and any h, at unit-variable cost, then a firm offering a good of quality $\bar{u} + \delta$, and any h, at a price $p + c(\bar{u} + \delta)$ will capture at least fraction μ of consumers.

We can in fact interpret A1 directly as follows: for any given quality increment, were the richest consumer offered that quality improvement in return for a price increase which covered *only* the *variable*-cost increment incurred in effecting that improvement, then he would strictly prefer the improved variety.

This assumption involves, then, an idea central to the vertical product differentiation literature. (Readers interested in pursuing that connection may like to compare this statement with the formulation in Shaked and Sutton 1983.)

We now turn to our second assumption which relates to the behaviour of *fixed costs*. Again we first state it in terms of our quality index, u.

A2: Let $F(u)$ be defined on $[0, \infty]$, and suppose that $F(u)$ is positive and increasing. Then we require that $F'(u)/F(u)$ is bounded above.

The reason why such an assumption is needed is as follows: what is at issue here is the question of how increases in market size (population of consumers) affect the equilibrium outcome. In fact, it turns out that as market size increases, the range of qualities on offer will tend to increase. What our assumption requires is that the proportionate increase in fixed costs required to achieve a given quality improvement is bounded.

Again, we can bypass the use of the quality indicator, and combine assumptions A1 and A2 in the following:

• There exists some factor k, such that by incurring k times more fixed cost than any other market participant, a firm can guarantee sales of μS at a mark-up p over unit-variable cost, irrespective of the price set by other firms.

In fact, k is equal to $e^{\beta\delta}$, in the terminology of assumptions 1 and 2.

We now state a proposition which implies that no 'limit-theorem' result of the kind explored in the preceding section can hold good in this context:

> Proposition 2: Under assumptions A1, A2, there exists some $\epsilon > 0$, such that at equilibrium at least one firm has a market share greater than ϵ irrespective of the size of the economy.

The above proposition states an extremely weak result. The point of developing it in this form is that it represents a very robust result in terms of the structure of the underlying oligopoly model. It can readily be shown that the result survives the following changes to the structure of the underlying model:

• Forms of price competition: replacing Bertrand competition by Cournot competition in the final stage of the game leaves the result unchanged.

• Design of the game: replacing simultaneous entry of firms by sequential entry also leaves the result unchanged.

• Multiproduct firms: the proposition also holds good if firms are allowed to produce a set of products with various (horizontal and vertical) attributes. (Denoting the number of products a firm offers by n, and the highest quality it offers as $\bar{u}$, the firm is assumed to incur fixed cost $F(\bar{u}) + (n - 1)\alpha$, where α is some positive constant.)

The result, then, is an unusually 'robust' one. Over a broad range of specifications of the underlying model we find that no 'convergence' to a fragmented structure is possible.

The intuition underlying this result is as follows: suppose we have a fragmented structure, in which a large number of firms each enjoys a small market share. The level of revenue earned by each firm will then be correspondingly small. As the size of the economy increases, the returns in terms of revenue which can be earned through an increase in 'quality' become larger relative to the fixed costs of achieving that 'quality' increase. This leads to a tendency for a 'fragmented' equilibrium to break down as (some) firms escalate their fixed outlays in order to outdistance the (possibly large) number of small firms present in the market.

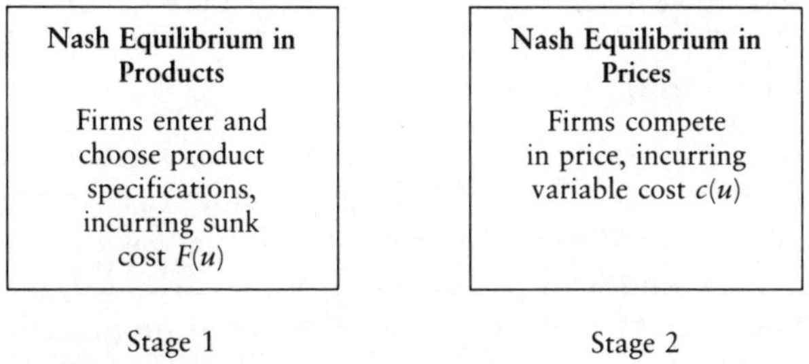

Nash Equilibrium in Products	Nash Equilibrium in Prices
Firms enter and choose product specifications, incurring sunk cost $F(u)$	Firms compete in price, incurring variable cost $c(u)$
Stage 1	Stage 2

Fig. 2.2 The 'Endogenous Fixed Cost' Model

3. Extensions

The proposition outlined in the preceding section underlines the fact that a fundamentally different mechanism comes into play once endogenous fixed costs are present. The model also suggests some further ideas whose development lies outside our present scope; here we indicate briefly some of these extensions.

Dual Structure

A fundamental feature of the model just described is that it permits the coexistence of a (relatively small) number of firms incurring relatively high levels of fixed costs, together with a (large) number of small firms who sell at lower prices and earn lower unit margins—but whose lower profits in 'stage 2' suffice to cover the lower level of fixed costs incurred at 'stage 1'.

In fact this kind of pattern is commonly observed within both R & D intensive and advertising-intensive industries. In the advertising context it is common to find a fringe of small producers who do no advertising and who sell exclusively in 'price-sensitive' market segments (in the food and drink sector, for example, they focus on industrial and catering sales, supplying 'own-label' products etc.).

The equilibria characterized above may be computed explicitly for the special case in which there are two classes of consumers who differ in their 'sensitivity to quality', U_u. The equilibrium configuration of products (firms) in this case corresponds to a 'dual' structure in which firms choose one or other of two advertising levels and so partition themselves into a 'small' number of 'high advertisers' and a 'large' number of 'low advertisers'. (Sutton 1989c)

Interaction with Set-Up Costs

An obvious extension of the above 'dual' model relates to the case where firms incur *both* exogenously given set-up costs in beginning production, *and* endogenous fixed costs associated with advertising or R & D expenditures. A treatment of this extended model lies outside our present scope. For a discussion of its properties, and an empirical investigation of its results, the reader is referred to Sutton 1989*c*.

4. Conclusions

We have been concerned in the present chapter with some basic features of models involving 'endogenous sunk costs'. Our main emphasis has been on drawing out a fundamental difference between these models, and models in which the level of sunk costs is exogenously determined. While the present characterization may seem a rather abstract one, these models none the less appear to offer a natural point of departure in re-examining many issues surrounding the relationship between scale economies, advertising, R & D and industrial structure.

References

Baumol, W. and Willig, D. (1981), 'Fixed Costs, Sunk Costs and Sustainability of Monopoly', *Quarterly Journal of Economics*, 96: 405–31.

Bonanno, G. (1987), 'Location Choice, Product Proliferation and Entry Deterrence', *Review of Economic Studies*, 54: 37–45.

Hallagan, W. and Joerding, W. (1983), 'Polymorphic Equilibrium in Advertising', *Bell Journal of Economics*, 14: 191–201.

Lane, W. (1980), 'Product Differentiation in a Market with Endogenous Sequential Entry', *Bell Journal of Economics*, 11: 237–60.

Schmalensee, R. (1978), 'Entry Deterrence in the Ready-to-Eat Breakfast Cereal Industry', *Bell Journal of Economics*, 9: 305–27.

Shaked, A. and Sutton, J. (1983), 'Natural Oligopolies', *Econometrica*, 51: 1469–84.

—— and —— (1987a), 'Product Differentiation and Industrial Structure', *Journal of Industrial Economics*, 36: 131–46.

—— and —— (1987b), 'Multiproduct Firms and Market Structure', ST/ICERD Working Paper No. 154, London School of Economics.

Sutton, J. (1986), 'Vertical Product Differentiation: Some Basic Themes', *American Economic Review, Papers and Proceedings*, 76: 393–8.

—— (1989a), 'Is Imperfect Competition Empirically Empty?' G. Feiwel (ed.), in *The Economics of Imperfect Competition and Employment: Joan Robinson and Beyond*, London: Macmillan.

—— (1989b), 'Endogenous Fixed Costs and the Structure of Advertising Intensive Industries', *European Economic Review*, 33:335–44.

—— (1989c), *Sunk Costs and Market Structure* (in preparation).

3

The Role of Potential Competition in Industrial Organization

Richard J. Gilbert

Potential competition has been recognized as a mechanism to control the exploitation of market power at least since the work of J. B. Clark (1902), but it was not until 50 years later that economists, most notably Joe Bain and Paolo Sylos-Labini, refocused attention on the idea. With inputs from the theories of imperfect competition, optimal control, and dynamic games, their work evolved into ever more sophisticated models of the reactions of existing competitors to the threat of new competition. Although the most appropriate models of competitive interaction are those which begin with a specific industry, a number of theories have been proposed which attempt to develop more general conclusions. My purpose in this paper is to develop an understanding of the strengths and limitations of these alternative theories by examining the available theoretical, empirical, and institutional knowledge.

Rather than attempt the Sisyphean task of recounting every model which relates conditions of entry and market performance, I have partitioned the analysis into four major schools of thought, according to their most central propositions. These are the traditional model of limit pricing, dynamic limit pricing, the theory of contestable markets, and the market efficiency model. Traditional limit pricing models rest on the assumption that firms respond to entry, but are able to earn persistent profits when the structural characteristics of markets make entry difficult. Dynamic limit pricing is similar, but emphasizes that markets can only be temporarily protected from entry. Contestability theory, in its pure form, asserts that potential competition is as effective as actual competition in controlling market performance. The efficient markets hypothesis, broadly interpreted, states that markets are workably competitive and that the market structure reflects differential efficiency, not strategic behaviour. While one can construct many other hypotheses about potential competition, these classifications are intended to span a broad range of predictions. This paper attempts to present testable conclusions that follow as consequences from these different schools of thought and to examine these conclusions in the light of available data.

A warning is appropriate here. This paper is not an attempt to provide a complete or balanced view of its subject. For example, the theory of contestable markets, developed by Baumol, Panzar, and Willig (1982), receives more than an equal share of attention in this paper. This uneven approach is motivated in part by the fact that the specific conclusions of the theory of perfectly contestable markets lend themselves to a critical review, and in part by the excitement and controversy that this theory has stirred in our profession.

Hypotheses About Entry

I will consider several alternative hypotheses that are intended to reflect prevailing theoretical views about the process and consequences of entry. I have intended these hypotheses to conform to prevailing theoretical models, but given the fact that little of the theory of entry prevention has been developed with the intention of providing empirically testable results, I regret that the correspondence between my hypotheses and specific models of entry prevention may be less than exact.

Hypothesis 1: Markets Behave According to the Classic Limit Pricing Model

I use the term 'Classic limit pricing model' to refer generally to the structural theory of market performance developed by Joe Bain and his contemporaries. Bain identified the 'conditions of entry' as technological features of markets that affect the exercise of market power. He identified economies of scale, absolute cost advantages, and product differentiation as the primary determinants of 'entry barriers', defined to be factors that enable an established firm to maintain price above average cost. While Bain considered these barriers to be partly exogenous, they clearly can be affected by the investments and technology chosen by firms.

The most straightforward application of the classical limit

pricing model is to pricing with economies of scale. An established firm (or group of firms) can prevent entry by producing enough so that if a new firm should enter, its additional output would force price to fall below its average cost. A central assumption in the limit pricing model is that entrants expect that established firms will not accommodate entry by reducing their output.[1] (I'll return to this assumption in the discussion of contestability theory.) Following Modigliani's (1958) formulation, the limit output is the smallest pre-entry output for which entry is not profitable. The corresponding limit price is the highest price at which entry is deterred, under the assumption that incumbents would maintain their pre-entry outputs if entry should occur. As Figure 3.1 illustrates, if an established firm can choose the level of output that it would maintain after entry, the firm can elevate price above average cost while presenting an entrant (with a similar technology) with no

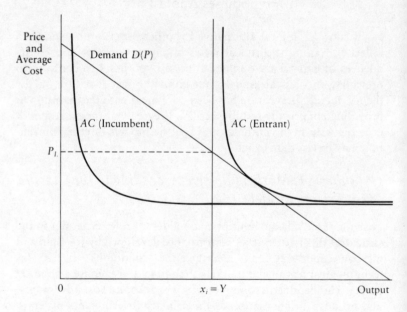

Fig. 3.1 Limit Pricing

[1] A particular example of the non-accommodation assumption is the 'Sylos postulate' that established firms will maintain their pre-entry outputs, named after the work of Sylos-Labini (1962, originally published in Italian in 1958). Game theorists will recognize this assumption as Nash-Cournot behaviour on the part of entrants, with the incumbent acting as a Stackelberg leader.

profitable market opportunity. With economies of scale, the limit price exceeds the minimum average cost of production and established firms earn persistent profits.

The limit pricing theory can be applied to other determinants of the conditions of entry, too. As Dixit (1979) has shown, an established firm with a differentiated product can follow a similar strategy to exploit consumer preferences when increasing returns are present in the production technology. With absolute cost advantages, the limit price is the (higher) average cost of an assumed disadvantaged entrant.

The particular formulation of the limit pricing model is not important for my purpose. What is important is the essential implication that established firms can exploit structural features of the market to earn persistent above-normal profits. Modest entry barriers could translate into large incumbent profits if entrants expect that entry would trigger aggressive price-cutting behaviour (Spence, 1977; Stiglitz, 1987). In the absence of a reputation for aggressive behaviour, an established firm wishing to deter entry would need a mechanism to signal to potential entrants that it will not act passively in response to an entry attempt. Dixit (1980) shows that sunk costs may offer such a mechanism. To the extent that an established firm has sunk investment expenditures and excess capacity, its marginal cost of production is lower than that of a new firm with the same technology (for which expenditures are not yet sunk). Thus, sunk costs can make operation at capacity profitable for an established firm challenged by new competition, even if competition lowers its marginal revenue. Other possible mechanisms include switching costs (Farrell and Shapiro, 1988; Gelman and Salop, 1983), product differentiation (Dixit, 1979), or pricing practices such as 'take or pay' requirements (Aghion and Bolton, 1987).

If equilibrium after entry is unaffected by the behaviour of incumbent firms before entry, there is no scope for limit pricing. In this case, entry will be prevented only if the market cannot sustain an additional firm when established firms act without regard to the effects of their behaviour on entry. (Bain would say that entry is 'blockaded' in this case.) However, if established firms can commit to actions that will make entry less profitable, they may choose to do so, provided the cost of these commitments does not exceed the profits that would be lost if entry occurs. If potential competitors use pre-entry price as a signal of post-entry profitability, incumbent firms may be forced to lower prices to prevent rivals from inferring that their markets are unduly profitable (Salop, 1979; Milgrom and Roberts, 1982).

There are many variants of the limit pricing model, but they all share a few distinguishing features. When limit pricing occurs, dominant firms will earn profits that persist above normal levels. Entry is generally followed by price competition and incumbent firms (approximately) maintain their pre-entry outputs.[2] Potential competition should have a moderating effect on industry profits, but it should not be as effective as actual competition in controlling pricing behaviour. Finally, if limit pricing is occurring, we should observe strategic behaviour designed to deter entry or to mitigate its consequences.

Hypothesis 2: Markets Follow the Dynamic Limit Pricing Model

In the classical limit pricing model, entry is an all or nothing affair. At a price below the limit price, the threat of entry is eliminated; at a price above the limit price, entry occurs instantaneously. In dynamic markets where scale or technical requirements do not restrict entry, however, a reservoir of nameless competitors may stand ready to spill into the industry at a rate that depends on expected profits. Knowing this, incumbent firms can trade off the current profitability against the prospect that high profits today will increase the rate at which new competition is attracted to the industry. When an established firm or cartel chooses a high price, competitive fringe producers increase their production and erode the cartel's market share. Geroski (1987) calls this 'optimally managed decline.'[3] In its simplest guise, it is the 'inverted umbrella'

[2] Although limit pricing is consistent with a range of incumbent responses to entry, we should not observe that established firms consistently reduce output to accommodate new entry.

[3] For example, as formulated by Gaskins (1971), a dominant firm chooses a price path (p_t) to maximize

$$\Pi(t_0) = \int_{t_0}^{T} (p_t - c) [D(p_t) - x_t] dt$$

where $D(p_t)$ is total demand at price p_t, x_t is the total supply from competing firms, and c is the dominant firm's average cost of production (taken to be constant). It is assumed that the rate of change of x_t is an increasing function of the price set by the dominant firm.

story of cartel pricing described by Stigler (1968). More sophisticated versions, which can include non-price competition, have been developed by Gaskins (1971), Kamien and Schwartz (1971), Friedman (1979), Judd and Peterson (1986), and others.

An internally consistent model of dynamic limit pricing can be difficult to specify. For example, it is not clear why the dominant firm should be a price leader, particularly after its market share has been eroded by entry. In the earlier dynamic limit pricing models, potential competitors were just an exogenously given force, responding to prices chosen by the dominant firm. Judd and Peterson (1986) derive entry from profit-maximizing behaviour, but they impose an exogenous cash constraint on new competitors.

But despite the limitations of theories of dynamic limit pricing, several distinctive conclusions emerge. Dominant firms will earn supranormal profits, but these profits will gradually erode. The gains from incumbency are transient. Furthermore, pricing behaviour should depend not only on interactions between established firms, but also on the threat of potential competition for the industry. Even as dominant firms decline, they are altering their behaviour to slow the rate at which they lose market share to new competitors.

Hypothesis 3: Markets are Perfectly Contestable

In its pure form, the theory of contestable markets developed by Baumol, Panzar, and Willig (1982) is not a description of firm behaviour but is rather a statement about the properties of equilibria in a certain kind of market. In a perfectly contestable market, industry prices and outputs are defined as 'sustainable' if no new firm (using the same technology as incumbent firms) can choose lower prices (for one or more of the products offered by existing firms) and operate profitably by serving all or part of demand at the new prices. Baumol–Panzar–Willig then define a contestable market as any market which can only be in equilibrium if the market price–quantity vector is sustainable.[4]

The definition, although not related to a particular description of

---

[4] Much criticism of contestability theory has focused on the extent to which sustainability is a feasible and necessary condition of market equilibria. It is not difficult to construct examples of markets in which sustainable price–quantity pairs do not exist. Most familiar models of imperfect competition, such as the Nash-Cournot model, generate equilibria that do not satisfy the conditions of sustainability.

a competitive process, is none the less elegant. In a perfectly contestable market equilibrium, total revenue must equal total cost. If revenues exceed costs, a new firm could enter at lower prices and still be profitable. If two or more firms operate in a contestable market, the price for each product that is sold must be equal to marginal cost, since any deviation of price from marginal cost would create opportunities for profitable marginal adjustments in the output(s) of one of the firms. Even if the market is a natural monopoly, if it is also perfectly contestable, price will be sufficient only to cover average cost. In such a situation contestability amounts to a perfect surrogate for price regulation under the constraint that the regulated firm must break even. With two or more firms, a perfectly contestable market replicates the equality of price and marginal cost in a perfectly competitive market.[5]

The concept of a perfectly contestable market does not rely on a description of firm behaviour. But when 'contestable market' is used in the active voice, it presumes the existence of 'hit and run' entrants who are able and willing to enter an industry whenever profit opportunities arise. Such entry makes sense only if the potential entrant has little at risk. According to Baumol and Willig (1986, p. 4), the theory accomplishes this by 'stripping away through its assumptions all barriers to entry and exit'.

Contestability becomes controversial when it moves from the theory with its assumption of zero entry barriers to situations where entry barriers are modest, but not absent. A key relationship is how quickly prices move in response to entry. Baumol *et al.* (1986) describe a model that reproduces some of the predictions of perfectly contestable markets with non-trivial barriers to entry, provided prices move slowly in response to entry. On the other hand, Farrell (1986*a*), Gilbert and Harris (1984), Gilbert (1986) and Stiglitz (1987) present models to show that if prices move quickly, established firms can maintain supranormal profits even if the sunk costs of entry are small. The key difference is that if prices

[5] A perfectly contestable market does not assure that the selection of products that are offered for sale will maximize total economic surplus subject to the break-even constraint. With economies of scale, there is a particular set of products that results in the largest economic surplus. Perfectly contestable market equilibria may exist with more than one set of products. Taking prices as given, an entrant firm may not be able to introduce the most efficient set of products without making losses. This would not be the case if firms were able to price discriminate, but contestability theory as formulated by Baumol, Panzar, and Willig (1982), assumes that firms are restricted to linear prices.

move quickly in response to entry, then hit and run entry becomes very risky if there are any sunk costs.

Perfect contestability has strong testable implications for market performance. If industry prices are sustainable, established firms will not earn profits that exceed or fall short of normal levels. If barriers to entry or exit are insignificant, profits will be held to negligible levels by the threat of potential entry alone. Incumbency has neither benefits nor costs. Firms will minimize costs subject to the constraint that revenues are sufficient to cover costs; they will not make investments that are inefficient at chosen levels of output, but are intended to deter entrants. If the cost-minimizing industry structure is independent of the number of firms in the industry, then entry or exit of a firm should have no effect on prices. Finally, prices should move slowly relative to the movement of capital into or out of a contestable industry.

Hypothesis 4: Efficiency Differences Explain Market Shares and Profit

I will describe this hypothesis as the 'Chicago school' of industrial organization, with apologies to those both within and outside the windy city who might be offended by this nomenclature. Without denying the importance of imperfect competition, the Chicago school represents that market evolution reflects differential efficiency. Dominant firms owe their position to superior performance, not to strategic behaviour or the history of entry into the industry, and profits are simply the rents that accrue to superior technology (Stigler, 1968, ch. 7; Demsetz, 1973). The Chicago school does not reject the concept of barriers to entry, but believes that they play a relatively minor role (Demsetz, 1982).

The unique perspective of the Chicago school can be illustrated by its definition of 'barriers to entry'. Stigler proposed that an entry barrier be limited to 'a cost of producing (at some or every rate of output) which must be borne by firms seeking to enter an industry but is not borne by firms already in the industry'. According to this definition, if both new and old firms have access to the same technology, the extent of scale economies is not a barrier to entry, as it affects equally the costs of both firms. This would be true even if scale economies limited the market to a single firm.

In the classic limit pricing model, remember, scale economies are an entry barrier because the model assumes that incumbents will maintain their outputs and thus constrain the market available to new entrants. If entrants believed they could compete on an equal footing with incumbents (which is implicit in the theory of perfectly contestable markets), scale economies would have no different effect on new entrants than on established firms. They would not be a barrier to entry. Thus, the key difference here is whether established firms can hold on to market share, and can communicate their ability to new entrants.

The Chicago school has not been structured as a formal model of potential competition, but with trepidation I will try to summarize its salient implications. Gains from incumbency should be modest and temporary. Strategic behaviour by established firms to affect the conditions of entry should be minimal. Industry structure and profits should reflect cost differences, not accidents of history that determine the order of entry of firms. Market concentration should not, by itself, be a determinant of prices.

In many respects, the Chicago school theory of markets is a weak form of the contestable markets hypothesis. Whereas entry barriers are non-existent in perfectly contestable markets, they play a minor and temporary role in the Chicago school. With two or more firms contestable markets act as if they are perfectly competitive. In the Chicago school, markets are 'workably' competitive.[6]

Empirical Evidence on Entry and Market Performance

There is no scarcity of reasonable theories of entry behaviour, but theory alone cannot answer the question of which of the many alternative models is the best predictor of entry behaviour. We must turn to the empirical evidence which bears on the assumptions and implications of the various hypotheses about entry.

Experimental Studies of Entry

Experimental economics provides a way to study alternative

[6] In principle, contestability could be generalized to make it more similar to the predictions of the Chicago school. Suppose firms had access to different technologies. Then the contestability result might imply that established firms are winners of a second price auction, in which the market price is determined by the next most efficient firm. Although a model with these properties has been described by Grossman (1981), there has been little attempt to apply this theory to actual markets.

hypotheses in settings that are highly structured, if not precisely controlled.[7] Broadly speaking, there are two types of relevant experiments. The first type examines whether a theory performs as expected when the experimental design conforms as closely as possible to both the structural and behavioural assumptions of the theory. This might require imposing specialized rules of the game, such as which competitor moves first and whether firms can commit to prices, which are not always present in actual competitive situations, but such confirming results are a minimal condition for any plausible theory. The second type of experiment does not impose behavioural assumptions other than what might naturally emerge from the structural assumptions of the theory. These experiments can offer practical insights as to the validity of the theory, but only to the extent that the experimental design reflects actual market conditions.

A good example of the first sort of experiment is provided by Harrison (1986), who performed experiments in which the rules of the game were structured to show contestability in its most favourable light. Sellers designated as incumbents were instructed to make public price offers which could not be changed in the subsequent period. Potential competitors faced no costs of entry and demand was simulated by computer, which removed any scope for strategic play by consumers. The institutional design in the Harrison experiment imposed a structure in which the incumbent firm has a first-mover advantage and potential competitors evaluate the profitability of entry with full knowledge of the price that will obtain if entry occurs. It should not be surprising that the outcome of the Harrison game was generally supportive of contestability. In most cases prices converged to average cost, which is also the price predicted by the theory for this market. Convergence to average cost did take some time and at least one case witnessed a successful attempt to maintain a collusive price, although this collusion was subsequently thwarted by introducing an additional seller.

The Harrison experiment was carefully designed to conform to the behavioural assumptions of contestability theory, and the results are supportive of that theory. Thus, the Harrison experiment showed that contestability theory is internally consistent when both the structural and behavioural assumptions of the model are replicated in the experiment.

---

[7] The following discussion parallels that in Schwartz (1986).

However, experiments which relax some of the assumptions behind contestability theory, or allow for sunk costs, offer little support for the hypothesis that potential competition can be as effective as actual competition in policing market behaviour.

Coursey, Isaac, and Smith (1984) ran a series of experiments comparing the outcomes of a monopoly market with the outcome of a duopoly with costless entry and exit. Production exhibited increasing returns to scale, so the efficient market structure called for a single firm. In each iteration of the experimental market, each firm was allowed to post a take-it-or-leave-it price at which deliveries would be made for quantities demanded, subject to the seller's capacity limit. Demand was specified in each experiment, but was not known to the sellers (except as revealed by purchase decisions). The authors reported that as the market was repeated, prices in the duopoly case tended to move closer to average cost than to the monopoly price.[8] They interpreted this result as support for a 'weak contestable markets' hypothesis: that prices, quantities, and market efficiency are closer to competitive than to monopoly levels.[9] However, the authors were not clear as to the process by which price moved towards average cost. If the experimental market replicated the predictions of the theory of perfectly contestable markets, a single firm would satisfy demand at a price equal to average cost, and entry would not occur. Coursey, Isaac, and Smith did not explain whether price movements reflected the outputs of both firms or the output of a single firm that was pricing to deter entry. This distinction is crucial to the validity of contestability theory.[10]

In a subsequent paper, Coursey, Isaac, Luke, and Smith (1984) describe the results of a series of market experiments similar to their earlier study, except for the introduction of sunk costs associated

[8] In these experiments, when a single firm supplies the entire market, average cost is equal to marginal cost because the firm is capacity constrained. Therefore the competitive price and the efficient price subject to non-negative profits are the same.

[9] Harrison and McKee (1985) conducted market experiments with a design similar to that in Coursey, Isaac, and Smith (1984) (no sunk costs, symmetric price offers). They also found that prices were closer to competitive than to monopoly levels, but they concluded that a system of regulation through franchise bidding was superior to market competition in limiting profits.

[10] In Table 1, Coursey, Isaac, and Smith (1984, p. 67) state the supply side of the contestable markets hypothesis as 'supply unrestricted at the competitive price by at least one firm'. But the prediction of the theory for their experimental design is supply at a price equal to average cost by only one firm.

with an entry decision. The experimental design provided for two firms, one established and the other a potential entrant. Entry required the purchase of a permit, which was valid for five periods, and the duopoly game was repeated for a total of twenty periods. When amortized over its useful life, the entry fee would have reduced the level of monopoly profits by 10 per cent.[11] As in the earlier paper, the authors conclude with support for a weak contestable markets hypothesis.

However, here it is more apparent that results of these experiments contradict an important prediction of the theory of contestable markets. In every repetition of the experiment, the potential entrant purchased an entry permit at least once (the entrant had four chances to enter, corresponding to the five period duration of the permit and the twenty period duration of the game). Yet entry was clearly inefficient in this experiment. Contestability theory would predict that the incumbent would price closest to average cost (excluding the entry fee) and there would be no entry. Potential, not actual, entry should police the pricing behaviour of the established firm. The authors refer to this outcome as 'limit pricing (contestable markets hypothesis)'. It did occur, but only at one point in one of the twelve experiments. In four of the twelve cases the incumbent was able to raise price significantly above average cost without triggering an entry decision at a point where entry was feasible. The authors refer to these examples as 'unstable pricing', but they are not inconsistent with limit pricing in which the established firm exploits the sunk cost of entry into the market.

These experiments do illustrate the limits of potential entry as a constraint on monopoly pricing. In eleven of the twelve cases, high prices are eroded by actual entry, even though entry is inefficient. In these experiments, attempts to extract monopoly profits are followed by the entry of new competition. But prices are controlled by actual entry, not by the threat of potential entry.[12]

[11] The experimental design is complicated by the fact that the incumbent pre-commits to an entry permit that lasts from period 1 to period 10, but thereafter is on an equal footing with the entrant.

[12] Comparing their results to an earlier set of experiments with no sunk costs, Coursey, Isaac, Luke, and Smith (1984, p. 82) conclude that 'the effect of an entry cost is to weaken support for the strong form of the contestable markets hypothesis', in that prices converge to average cost in fewer cases. But once entry occurs, sunk costs should be irrelevant (except, perhaps for any role they might play in the formation of reputations).

Although economic experiments can sharpen our understanding, only the real world can test the ultimate validity of our models. In what follows, I will draw on industry studies about various aspects of competitive behaviour and market performance that bear on the alternative theories of entry described earlier.

The Existence and Persistence of Industry Profits

Joe Bain (1956) made the first systematic attempt to uncover a correlation between measures of market concentration, the conditions of entry, and monopoly profits. Bain identified a positive correlation between profits and both concentration and estimates of the height of barriers to entry, which he categorized as scale economies, absolute cost advantages, and product differentiation. In the absence of substantial barriers to entry, the correlation between profits and market concentration was weak, an observation which lends some support to the contestable market hypothesis.

Bain's studies were highly influential and his correlations have withstood repeated observations, in particular the importance of product differentiation in consumer products industries (Comanor and Wilson, 1967, among others). But Bain's investigations suffered from important deficiencies. The measurement of entry barriers was necessarily subjective and vulnerable to the criticism of circularity: are barriers high in industries that have persistent profits, or vice versa? Since accounting profits can differ widely from economic profits—for example, in the choice of depreciation schedules and the use of historical asset values—profitability itself is difficult to measure.

Several authors have attempted to estimate the magnitude and persistence of industry profits in other ways. Orr (1974) and Masson and Shaanan (1986) use the relationship between aggregate entry and exit and industry profitability as a means to estimate the importance of barriers to entry. Their estimates of 'hurdle profit rates', above which entry becomes significant, can be interpreted as measures of the height of entry barriers in different industries. Mueller (1986; 1977) found that profit levels in a sample of 600 of the largest US manufacturing corporations showed a strong tendency to revert over time to the sample mean, but the process was very slow. Estimated long run profits for the 100 companies with the highest profit levels in 1950 exceeded the sample average by more than 30 per cent.

These findings would be consistent with the contestability hypothesis only if the observed profitability figures were accounting artifacts; otherwise these persistent profits should be quickly eliminated. Even if accounting profits are only roughly correlated with economic profits, contestability would predict large changes in market shares in response to even small changes in profitability, and this is not revealed in the data.

Industry studies lend some credence to the classical limit pricing model, since the available data suggests that entry into new industries has been very difficult. In Masson and Shaanan's (1982) sample of 37 US industries over the period 1950–66, new entrants achieved an average market share penetration of only 4.5 per cent. Similar studies by Biggadike (1979), Yip (1982) and Hause and Du Reitz (1984) also revealed only modest share gains by new entrants.

Yet the evidence is that new competitors do move into markets and excess profits do not last indefinitely, although the decay rate is quite long. Whatever causes these persistent profits, competitive forces tend to eliminate them over time. Limit pricing is not a perfect tool for blocking new entrants. If structural features of industries are the main cause of limited entry, these barriers are eventually worn down and overcome.

Thus, these inter-industry studies are inconsistent with the theory of perfectly contestable markets, but they do not provide much conclusive evidence for any of the other theories of entry behaviour. Depending on one's view of how soon is soon enough, the evidence need not contradict either the classical limit pricing model or the model of dynamic limit pricing. The data are not sufficiently detailed to show whether established firms adjust their price (and/ or non-price) behaviour to moderate the threat of entry, or whether entry simply reflects the development of new managerial and technical skills, which would be consistent with the Chicago school. The dismal performance record of new entrants casts a shadow on the strict view that the evolution of market structure is driven *only* by technological efficiencies with *no* scope for incumbency advantages, but that description of the determinants of market structure probably exaggerates the view of even hard-core Chicagoans.[13]

---

[13] For example, Demsetz (1982) attributes informational and reputational advantages of early entrants as part of the costs of doing business and not barriers to entry. But Farrell (1986*b*) argues that such factors can work decidedly against new entrants.

Strategic Behaviour

Strategic behaviour to deter entry is an activity that intentionally compromises productive efficiency to protect an established market. To the extent that established firms strategically choose products, locations, outputs, advertising, R. & D. or other competitive actions that are motivated primarily by their consequences for entry, rather than by efficiency considerations, this behaviour contradicts both the perfectly contestable market and the Chicago school hypotheses.[14]

Do established firms actually engage in activities that are designed to protect their markets against entry? An enormous economics literature has examined the theoretical scope for strategic entry deterrence. Corporate strategy, including lessons in entry deterrence, has become a standard component of business school curricula. The business trade press cites product development and marketing strategies that are designed to improve the security of competitive niches, and court cases allege anticompetitive abuses against frustrated entrants. But this combination of anecdotal evidence is not a reliable index of how often strategic entry deterrence is attempted or how often it works.

The empirical literature gives mixed signals on the importance of strategic entry deterrence. Gilbert and Lieberman (1987) found that firms in concentrated chemical product industries could pre-empt the expansion of rival established firms by investing in new capacity, but it wasn't possible, from the available data, to discern whether such behaviour is intentional or profitable. Moreover, Lieberman (1987) did not find evidence to support pre-emptive capacity expansion designed to deter new entry. A possible explanation for Lieberman's results is the difficulty of committing to entry-deterring investment. Gilbert (1986) found that the technological characteristics of most industries are such that a single established firm could not commit to a production level that prevented entry, even if it had the desire to do so. For most industries, the fact that some costs are sunk is not sufficient for a single firm to maintain observed levels of output, and this is a necessary condition to deter entry.

[14] Of course, the line between deterring entry and efficiency is not always clear. It is possible that entry prevention results in outcomes that are more efficient than when entry is accommodated by established firms, and actions that are economically efficient may have incidental deterrence effects (von Weizsäcker, 1980; Demsetz, 1982).

Brand proliferation is commonly cited as another instrument to deter entry, as in the models of Schmalensee (1978) and Bonanno (1987). However, Judd (1985) argues that brand proliferation invites the entry of specialized firms, because the incumbent has an incentive to rearrange its product slate to accommodate an entrant. (See Gilbert and Matutes, 1989 for an attempt to reconcile these two opposing views.) A related strategy is spatial pre-emption. West (1981) examines the pattern of store location by competing supermarkets and concludes that deterrence is a factor in location choice.

Taken together, these studies constitute only fragile evidence that established firms take potential entry into account when developing their competitive policies. Clearly, given the popularity of models of strategic behaviour and their central role in the literature on potential competition, more work is needed to confirm or reject this proposition.

Industry Responses to Entry

Different theoretical models of potential entry make different assumptions about what new competitors expect to happen if they enter a market. But what responses have actually confronted new entrants in the past?

Yip (1982) surveyed managers in markets that experienced entry over the period 1972–9. Out of 69 instances of entry, Yip selected 36 which he judged to be most successful. These included 21 by direct investment and 15 by acquisition. Managers in the industries that were challenged by these entrants reported that only 29 per cent of the entries were viewed as 'serious' threats when they occurred. Only 30 per cent reported that they responded to entry with price competition, and then only in the case of direct entry, rather than when new management takes over an existing firm.[15] The failure to respond to entry with price competition is not inconsistent with contestability theory or the Chicago school. In a perfectly contestable market, if demand and technological conditions do not change, incumbents should not be expected to take entrants seriously because entry would not be viable.

[15] None of the alternative theories presented here predicts the consequences for industry performance of a change in management, in the absence of a change in industry concentration. Given the prevalence of entry by acquisition of existing assets, this is an important deficiency.

But Yip's data should be interpreted with caution. They are subjective, and the meaning of a 'competitive response' is not well-defined. Since they pertain only to the most successful entrants, their success could be a direct consequence of the reluctance of managers of incumbent firms to take the entrants seriously when they first entered the industry. Furthermore, managers might be reluctant to describe their competitive strategies in much detail.

Lieberman (1987) examined how incumbent firms in 39 chemical product industries responded to entry by estimating equations specifying investment rates for established firms and new entrants. He found that entry into industries characterized by relatively high concentration levels was typically followed by an expansion of capacity by the incumbent firms. Incumbent firms in concentrated industries did not respond positively to expansion by other incumbents, and incumbents in relatively unconcentrated industries did not increase their investment activity in response to new entry.

Lieberman's results are consistent with Caves and Porter's (1977) theory of 'mobility deterrence'. Incumbent firms (in the relatively concentrated industries in Lieberman's sample) invest to retard the rate of growth of new entrants, but they do not necessarily invest to prevent entry. In an economy with stationary technology and demand, these observations are inconsistent with the contestable market and the Chicago school hypotheses. In an otherwise stationary environment, these models predict that successful entry should coincide with lower output or exit of an incumbent firm. These observations are also inconsistent with common formulations of dynamic limit pricing, in which established firms accommodate entry by reducing their own output in response to production increases by competitive 'fringe' firms. Also rejected is the Sylos postulate that established firms will maintain their pre-entry outputs, but an increase in output by established firms is not inconsistent with credible limit pricing, as Bulow, Geanakoplos, and Klemperer (1985) explain in discussing Dixit's (1980) limit pricing model.

However, these conclusions from Lieberman's results depend on the assumption of a stationary environment. One might expect entry to coincide with advances in technology or with new information that leads to optimistic expectations of demand growth. In either case, one would expect that both entrants and incumbent firms would react with greater output, so that entrant and incumbent capacity expansion would be positively correlated. However, Lieberman does not find this positive correlation in industries with relatively low concentration levels.

Bresnahan and Reiss (1987) take a different approach to the measurement of incumbent responses to entry. They restrict their set of observations to markets (primarily services in rural areas) that can support no more than a few firms, which allows them to isolate the competitive effects of a discrete entry decision. By examining a cross-section of markets they are able to estimate a critical market size at which monopoly profits are sufficient to support a single firm. In the same way, they estimate a critical market size that can just support two firms in the same market. Bresnahan and Reiss argue that if firms are equally efficient and if entry does not result in price cutting, then the size of the market that supports two firms should be about twice as large as the size of the market that just supports one firm. However, if entry results in aggressive price competition, then for two firms to survive, the market would have to be more than twice as large as the market that can support a single firm. Their empirical results show a range in the ratio of the critical market size for two firms and for one firm, varying from about two to four. These results suggest that at least in some markets, established firms respond aggressively to entry, which lowers the profit an entrant can expect and should act as a deterrent to potential competitors.[16]

The findings of Bresnahan and Reiss (1987) are consistent with the implications of the classical limit pricing model. Both contestability theory and the Chicago school imply that demand conditions should not adversely affect a second entrant into a market, yet these results suggest otherwise.

Benefits to Incumbency

Much of the preceding discussion was targeted to the question of whether established firms earn persistent, above-normal profits. A related but distinct question is whether these persistent profits

---

[16] Some of the Bresnahan and Reiss findings are counterintuitive. For example, the ratio was highest for veterinarians and lowest for auto dealers, while casual observations on the extent of rivalry might suggest the opposite. A difficulty with their approach is that their market measures are static, whereas entry should depend on the present value of profit streams that can be earned in a market. Bresnahan and Reiss measure only current market size, not present value profits, and the relationship between the two can be tenuous.

result from incumbency, or some other factor. For example, some industries may experience high rates of growth in demand or technological progress that contribute to sustained profits above normal levels. However, if established firms and recent entrants earn similar profits, it would be difficult to conclude that the high profits are a result of incumbency.

Urban, Carter, Gaskin, and Mucha (1984) examined 129 frequently purchased consumer brands in 12 US markets. They found that market shares were a decreasing function of the order of the entry of the brand. Early entrants enjoyed larger market shares, all else equal. Large market shares need not imply higher profitability, but the study does suggest that the history of entry into an industry produces some asymmetry in the condition of firms.

Contestability theory predicts that no rents are derived from incumbency. An incumbent firm can protect a natural monopoly, but it cannot earn rents as a result. In addition, the sequence of entry into a market should not, by itself, account for differences in profits or market shares, as all firms are presumed to have access to the same technology.

However, the empirical evidence from Urban, Carter, Gaskin, and Mucha is not inconsistent with the weaker hypothesis of the Chicago school, if it happens that earlier entrants tend to be better able to satisfy consumer demands and therefore have higher market shares.

Entry in Deregulated Markets

Alfred Kahn once characterized the airlines as 'marginal costs on wings'. Indeed, sunk costs are small relative to total expenditures in the airline industry, the capital costs of entry into the industry are relatively low and the main component of fixed plant, the aircraft, is extraordinarily mobile and can be put to use in alternative markets in response to changing market conditions. Thus, many expected that the deregulated US airline industry would become the classic example of the effectiveness of the contestability thesis, with industry performance determined more by the threat of entry than by actual competitive circumstances.

This sanguine view was expressed by Bailey and Panzar (1981) shortly after the passage of the Airline Deregulation Act of 1978.

Although their findings were qualified by the limited evidence that became available between deregulation and the date of their study, they concluded that potential competition from the major trunk carriers was sufficient to police monopoly pricing behaviour in long-haul local markets (greater than 400 miles), but not in local markets of shorter distances where specialized equipment requirements make them less vulnerable to entry. They also concluded that equipment availability limited the effectiveness of potential competition in controlling pricing by trunk carriers.

Subsequent studies of competitive conditions in the US airline industry have generally praised the results of deregulation, but find little support for contestability theory in airline pricing behaviour. Airline route prices are sensitive to actual market concentration levels and prices have responded rapidly to entry and exit. There is widespread price discrimination for apparently similar services. The industry has evolved into a network of major hubs where a few airlines account for a major share of enplanements at each airport and entry of new competitors into these hubs has proved difficult (Maldutis, 1987).

Call and Keeler (1985) estimated a model of how fares were determined in major city-pair markets, including as explanatory variables the level of concentration in the market, the estimated elasticity of demand, and the entry of new carriers. They concluded that fares tend to be high in markets where concentration is high and estimated demand elasticity is low, and that incumbent carriers price aggressively in response to entry. Similarly, Bailey, Graham, and Kaplan (1984) found that fares levels were positively correlated with the degree of market concentration and that average fares in markets served by newly certified carriers were 20 per cent lower than in similar markets that did not experience entry of new carriers.

Call and Keeler used these observations and the behaviour of restricted and unrestricted fares to evaluate the predictive power of several alternative models of oligopoly behaviour, including contestability theory, dynamic limit pricing, and a variant of classical limit pricing emphasizing differentiated products.[17] The authors reject the hypothesis that airline markets were contestable

---

[17] The variant on limit pricing was the 'fat cat' model in Fudenberg and Tirole (1984). Models with similar consequences include Farrell and Shapiro (1988) and Gelman and Salop (1983).

over the period they studied.[18] They found support for pricing behaviour reflective of dynamic limit pricing, concluding (p. 243) that 'the evidence strongly supports the hypothesis that unrestricted fares have fallen on high-density routes, and that the fall has not been immediate, but gradual, occurring with the entry of new and existing firms on to new routes.' However, this finding is only partial support for dynamic limit pricing, because it shows only that entry took time and not that established firms adjusted their pricing to retard entry. Call and Keeler also found support for a variant of classical limit pricing exploiting product differentiation barriers to entry.

Using data collected over a longer post-deregulation time period, Morrison and Winston (1987) also conclude that airline pricing does not support the contestability hypothesis. Rather than looking at the effects of entry as in Call and Keeler (1985), Morrison and Winston focus on the role of potential competitors, which they define as carriers that serve at least one of the two airports in a particular city-pair route but do not serve that route. These carriers should have relatively small sunk costs of entry and exit. They found that the existence of potential competitors did act to control prices, but the effect was not as large as the control influenced by actual competitors, and prices tended to be above competitive levels. Their findings offered strong support for the classical model of limit pricing. Potential competition matters, but established firms are able to exploit barriers to entry and maintain prices above competitive levels.[19]

These studies and the observations in Kahn (1988) provide generous evidence that incumbent airline carriers typically re-

[18] The correlation between prices and concentration is not, by itself, a rejection of contestability theory. For example, some markets could be natural monopolies while others are natural oligopolies, and the (perfectly contestable) price could be higher in the first instance. Also, shifts in demand or technology can change a market from a natural monopoly to a natural duopoly, with a lower (perfectly contestable) price. Then entry would correlate with lower prices, even if the market is contestable. (I am grateful to John Panzar for this observation.) However, Call and Keeler's observed significance of demand elasticity is not consistent with contestability theory, and the observations on entry and exit suggest that the price movements reflect competition and not technology. Moreover, Caves, Christensen, and Tretheway (1984) find constant returns to scale for trunk and local carriers.

[19] Peteraf (1988) also suggests that potential competition has not affected pricing behaviour in the way expected by contestability theory. Specifically, potential competition was not observed to be more effective in situations where the sunk costs associated with entry are less.

sponded to the entry of aggressive carriers by selectively cutting prices on those routes which were challenged, and typically the competition took the particular form of lower prices for restricted travel. The industry went through periods of price-cutting that, in Kahn's opinion, were not sustainable. Industry profitability experienced wide swings, a result that is inconsistent with free entry and exit.

The industry has experienced a massive restructuring since deregulation in 1978. Entry occurred on a large scale, followed by bankruptcies and mergers. Low cost carriers forced reorganization by the major carriers. The structure of airline service changed to a 'hub and spoke' travel network. These changes make it more difficult to reach conclusions about the role of potential entry, but we know enough to suggest serious defects in contestability theory as it might apply to the airlines. For example, Call and Keeler found that entry into new markets by trunk airlines depressed prices in much the same way as entry by non-trunks, despite the fact that the trunks should have cost structures that are similar to the costs of established firms. Deregulation has brought an increasing awareness of the importance of sunk costs and other factors that limit the effectiveness of potential entry in the industry. These include ground support facilities (both cost and availability) and marketing innovations such as the frequent flyer programme which increase brand loyalty. There are also indications that control of computerized reservation systems is a factor in the ability of an airline to achieve success in new markets (US Department of Transportation, 1988).

The present hub and spoke organization of the airline market is consistent with the conclusion that potential competition is only partially effective in this industry, and thus not consistent with the theory of contestable markets. Market concentration at airport hubs is typically high, and the dominant firms at these hubs appear to enjoy market power that is not controlled by potential competition (Borenstein, 1988; 1989). It also casts doubt on the model of dynamic limit pricing, where a steady flow of entry slowly but surely erodes the market power of established firms. With the evidence that was available in 1985, Call and Keeler concluded that entry would eventually undermine any substantial exercise of market power in the airline industry. Later findings do not support this conclusion. The long run behaviour of the industry may be more indicative of the limit pricing model, where scale and product differentiation barriers to entry translate into persistent advantages for incumbent firms.

A Summing Up

Potential competition is important as a mechanism to control market power, as was observed by Clark, Bain, Sylos-Labini, and others. But these scholars considered potential competition to be an imperfect control. With the theory of perfectly contestable markets, potential competitors were elevated to a status comparable to that of actual competitors. In the theory of contestability, potential competition is an almost perfect control on monopoly power, the qualification being that price will equal average cost with potential competition, whereas price will equal marginal cost with actual competition in contestable markets. The observations presented here suggest that potential competition is important, but not as powerful as the theory of contestable markets implies.

With the diverse observations available and the rather loose connection between theoretical models and testable hypotheses, one can search for and find some support to bolster almost any theory of behaviour with potential competition. This should be expected, since the circumstances of each industry are unique and models that explain competitor behaviour in one industry may be inappropriate to describe behaviour in another. Yet, one function of economics is to make testable generalizations about economic behaviour, and in this role we have a responsibility to draw conclusions that apply as accurate generalizations, if not in every individual situation.

My strongest conclusions focus on the general validity of the model of perfectly contestable markets. There is only weak evidence consistent with this theory, and the amount of inconsistent evidence is substantial. In fairness to the proponents of the contestable markets theory, it was developed under the assumption that entry and exit are free, and tests of the theory should recognize this condition. Adherents of contestability theory can argue that many of the observations discussed in this paper are irrelevant to the theory because no one expects industries with substantial entry costs to be contestable. But a theory that applies only when entry and exit costs are strictly zero is of little practical value. The central question is whether contestability theory makes useful predictions about markets that are close to being perfectly contestable.

The experimental evidence provides some support for contestability theory, but the support depends on careful specification of strategies for the market participants. When strategies are not so tightly constrained, the experiments show only that competition is effective in controlling monopoly prices when entry barriers are small, a conclusion that follows from any of the models considered here. The specific conclusion of contestability theory—that potential competition is as good as actual competition—is not clearly supported by the outcomes of market experiments.

Airline markets were expected to have relatively low entry and exit costs, and with their availability of data, they have been a popular testing ground for the theory of contestable markets. Here again, most of the studies cast doubts on the theory. Although sunk costs may be relatively low for airlines, the validity of contestability theory also depends on the assumption that prices move slowly relative to capital. The speed with which airline competitors can respond to pricing initiatives, along with other factors that limit entry at airports and encourage brand recognition, have undermined the recent effectiveness of potential entry in this industry. These observations do not invalidate the theory of contestable markets, but they do suggest that different examples are needed to illustrate how the theory is relevant to actual markets.

The evidence is much less conclusive among the other competing theories of potential entry, which probably results from the large variation in the conditions of entry across industries. A host of studies find that some industries change in ways that are consistent with the dynamic limit pricing model. Profits are eroded over time as new entry occurs, but the success rate of new entrants is low and above-normal profits persist for a long time. These observations could also be construed as consistent with the classical limit pricing model. The Chicago school can't be dismissed either, because evidence that established firms act strategically to discourage entry is more anecdotal than actual.

It should be all too clear that despite a large body of data, the need for further empirical work in this area is abundant. But what is needed is rather different from the focus of most of the empirical work to date. Most existing studies have concentrated on the magnitude of entry and exit and the persistence of profits. Instead, what is needed is a better understanding of competitive behaviour in the presence of potential competition. Economists need to learn more about the extent to which price and non-price behaviour of established firms is conditioned on the threat of potential entry. Do new entrants respond to past episodes of entry and to the present strategies of established firms? Are potential entrants affected by the behaviour of established firms as assumed in the classical limit pricing model? Both contestability theory and the Chicago school implicitly assume that present prices are good indicators of post-entry profitability. When are these assumptions valid?

Progress has been made on these fronts, with recent advances coming from the study of specific industries, such as airlines, where the responses to competitive strategies can be examined in microscopic detail. Continued research that integrates theoretical models of competitive strategy with industry-level observations should be a productive tool in understanding the real potential of potential competition.

Acknowledgements

This paper relies in part on joint work with Paul Geroski and Alexis Jacquemin, reported in Geroski, Gilbert, and Jacquemin (forthcoming). I am grateful for their collaboration, and to Giacomo Bonanno, Severin Borenstein, Ted Keeler, John Panzar, Pierre Regibeau, and the editors of the *Journal of Economic Perspectives* for helpful discussions.

(This chapter appeared as an article in the *Journal of Economic Perspectives*, vol. 3, No. 3, Summer 1989, 107–128, and is reproduced by kind permission of the Journal.)

References

Aghion, P., and Bolton, P. (1987), 'Entry Prevention through Contracts with Customers', *American Economic Review*, 1987, 77.

Bailey, E., Graham, D., and Kaplan, D. (1984), *Deregulating the Airlines: An Economic Analysis*, Cambridge, MIT Press.

Bailey, E., and Panzar, John (1981), 'The Contestability of Airline Markets During the Transition to Deregulation', *Law and Contemporary Problems*, 44, 125–45.

Bain, J. (1956), *Barriers to New Competition*, Cambridge, Harvard University Press.

Baumol, William, Panzar, John, and Willig, R. (1982), *Contestable Markets and the Theory of Industry Structure*, New York, Harcourt, Brace, Jovanovich.

Baumol, William, Panzar, John, and Willig, Robert (1986), 'On the Theory of Perfectly-Contestable Markets', in Stiglitz, Joseph E., and Mathewson, F. eds., *New Developments in the Analysis of Market Structure*, Cambridge, MIT Press.

Baumol, William, and Willig, Robert (1986), 'Contestability: Developments Since the Book', in Morris, D. J., *et al.*, eds., *Strategic Behaviour and Industrial Competition*, Oxford, Clarendon Press.

Biggadike, E. (1979), *Corporate Diversification: Entry, Strategy and Performance*, Boston, Division of Research, Graduate School of Business Administration, Harvard University.

Bonanno, G. (1987), 'Location Choice, Product Proliferation and Entry Deterrence', *Review of Economics Studies*, 54, 37–45.

Borenstein, S. (1988), 'Hubs and High Fares: Airport Dominance and Market Power in the US Airline Industry', Institute of Public Policy Studies Discussion Paper No. 278, University of Michigan.

Borenstein, S. (1989), 'The Competitive Advantage of a Dominant Airline', Institute of Public Policy Studies Discussion Paper No. 280, University of Michigan.

Bresnahan, Timothy, and Reiss, P. (1987), 'What Kinds of Markets Have Too Few Firms?,' working paper, Stanford University.

Bulow, Jeremy, Geanakoplos, John, and Klemperer, Paul (1985), 'Holding Idle Capacity to Deter Entry', *Economic Journal*, 95, 178–82.

Call, G. and Keeler, T. (1985), 'Airline Deregulation, Fares, and Market Behaviour: Some Empirical Evidence', in Daugherty, A., ed., *Analytical Studies in Transport Economics*, Cambridge, Cambridge University Press.

Caves, Douglas, Christensen, Laurits, and Tretheway, Michael (1984),

'Economies of Density versus Economies of Scale: Why Trunk and Local Service Airline Costs Differ', *Rand Journal of Economics*, 15, 471–89.

Caves, R., and Porter, M. (1977), 'From Entry Barriers to Mobility Barriers: Conjectural Decisions and Contrived Deterrence to New Competition', *Quarterly Journal of Economics*, 97, 247–61.

Clark, J. B. (1902), *The Control of Trusts*, New York, Macmillan.

Comanor, William S., and Wilson, T. (1967), 'Advertising, Market Structure and Performance', *Review of Economic Studies*, 49, 423–40.

Coursey, Don, Isaac, R. Mark, and Smith, Vernon L. (1984), 'Market Contestability in the Presence of Sunk (Entry) Costs', *Rand Journal of Economics*, 15, 69–84.

Coursey, Don, Isaac, R. Mark, and Smith, Vernon L. (1984), 'Natural Monopoly and Contested Markets: Some Experimental Results', *Journal of Law and Economics*, 27, 91–113.

Demsetz, Harold (1973), 'Industry Structure, Market Rivalry and Public Policy', *Journal of Law and Economics*, 16, 1–9.

Demsetz, Harold (1982), 'Barriers to Entry', *American Economic Review*, 72, 47–57.

Dixit, Avinash (1979), 'A Model of Duopoly Suggesting a Theory of Entry Barriers,' *Bell Journal of Economics*, 10, 20–32.

Dixit, Avinash (1980), 'The Role of Investment in Entry Deterrence', *Economic Journal*, 90, 95–106.

Farrell, Joseph (1986a), 'How Effective is Potential Competition?', *Economics Letters*, 20, 67–70.

Farrell, Joseph (1986b), 'Moral Hazard as an Entry Barrier', *Rand Journal of Economics*, 17, 440–9.

Farrell, Joseph, and Shapiro, Carl (1988), 'Dynamic Competition with Switching Costs', *Rand Journal of Economics*, 19, 123–37.

Friedman, J., 'On Entry Preventing Behaviour and Limit Price Models of Entry', in Brams, S., Schotter, A., and Schwodiauer, G. eds. (1979), *Applied Game Theory*, Vienna, Springer.

Fudenberg, Drew, and Tirole, Jean (1984), 'The Fat-Cat Effect, the Puppy-Dog Ploy, and the Lean and Hungry Look', *American Economic Review: Papers and Proceedings*, 74, 361–66.

Gaskins, Darius W. Jr. (1971), 'Dynamic Limit Pricing: Optimal Pricing Under Threat of Entry', *Journal of Economic Theory*, 2, 306–22.

Gelman, Judith R., and Salop, Steven (1983), 'Capacity Limitation and Coupon Competition', *Bell Journal of Economics*, 14, 315–25.

Geroski, P. (1987), 'Do Dominant Firms Decline?' in Hay, D., and Vickers, J., eds., *The Economics of Market Dominance*, Oxford, Basil Blackwell.

Geroski, P., Gilbert, Richard J., and Jacquemin, A. (forthcoming), 'Barriers to Entry and Strategic Competition', in Sonnenschein, Hugo, and Lesourne, Jacques, *Fundamentals of Pure and Applied Economics: Encyclopedia of Economics*, Harwood Academic Publishers.

Gilbert, Richard J. (1986), 'Pre-emptive Competition', in Stiglitz, Joseph E., and Mathewson, F., eds., *New Developments in the Analysis of Market Structure*, Cambridge, MIT Press, 90–125.

Gilbert, Richard J., and Harris, Richard G. (1984), 'Competition with Lumpy Investment', *Rand Journal of Economics*, 15, 197–212.

Gilbert, Richard J., and Lieberman, M. (1987), 'Investment and Co-ordination in Oligopolistic Industries', *Rand Journal of Economics*, 18, 17–33.

Gilbert, Richard J., and Matutes, C. (1989), 'Product Line Rivalry with Brand Differentiation,' working paper, University of California.

Grossman, Sanford J. (1981), 'Nash Equilibrium and the Industrial Organization of Markets with Large Fixed Costs', *Econometrica*, 49, 1149–72.

Harrison, Glenn W. (1986), 'Experimental Evaluation of the Contestable Markets Hypothesis', in Bailey, E., ed., *Public Regulation*, Cambridge, MIT Press.

Harrison, Glenn W., and McKee, Michael (1985), 'Monopoly Behaviour, Decentralized Regulation, and Contestable Markets: An Experimental Evaluation', *Rand Journal of Economics*, 16, 51–69.

Hause, John C., and du Reitz, Gunnar (1984), 'Entry, Industry Growth and the Microdynamics of Industry Supply', *Journal of Political Economy*, 92, 733–57.

Judd, Kenneth L. (1985), 'Credible Spatial Pre-emption', *Rand Journal of Economics*, 16, 153–66.

Judd, Kenneth L., and Peterson, B. (1986), 'Dynamic Limit Pricing and Optimal Finance', *Journal of Economic Theory*, 39, 368–99.

Kahn, A. E. (1988), 'Surprises of Airline Deregulation', *American Economic Review: Papers and Proceedings*, 78, 316–22.

Kamien, Morton I., and Schwartz, Nancy L. (1971), 'Limit Pricing and Uncertain Entry', *Econometrica*, 39, 441–54.

Lieberman, M. (1987), 'Post-Entry Investment and Market Structure in the Chemical Processing Industries', *Rand Journal of Economics*, 18, 533–49.

Maldutis, J. (1987), 'Airline Competition at the Fifty Largest US Airports', Salomon Brothers, Inc.

Masson, Robert, and Shaanan, Joseph (1982), 'Stochastic Dynamic Limit Pricing: An Empirical Test', *Review of Economics and Statistics*, 64, 413–23.

Masson, Robert, and Shaanan, Joseph (1986), 'Excess Capacity and Limit Pricing: An Empirical Test', *Economica*, 53, 365–78.

Milgrom, Paul, and Roberts, John (1982), 'Limit Pricing and Entry Under Incomplete Information: An Equilibrium Analysis', *Econometrica*, 50, 443–59.

Modigliani, Franco (1958), 'New Developments on the Oligopoly Front', *Journal of Political Economy*, 66, 215–32.

Morrison, S., and Winston, C. (1987), 'Empirical Implications and Tests of the Contestability Hypothesis', *Journal of Law and Economics*, 30, 53–66.

Mueller, Dennis C. (1977), 'The Persistence of Profits above the Norm', *Economica*, 44, 369–80.

Mueller, D. C. (1986), *Profits in the Long Run*, Cambridge, Cambridge University Press.

Omori, Takashi, and Yarrow, George (1982), 'Product Diversification, Entry Prevention and Limit Pricing', *Bell Journal of Economics*, 13, 242–8.

Orr, Dale (1974), 'An Index of Entry Barriers and Its Application to the Market Structure Performance Relationship', *Journal of Industrial Economics*, 23, 39–49.

Pakes, A. (1987), 'Mueller's "Profits in the Long Run" ', *Rand Journal of Economics*, 18, 319–32.

Peteraf, M. (1988), 'Contestability in Monopoly Airline Markets', Northwestern University Discussion Paper No. 10.

Salop, Steven (1979), 'Strategic Entry Deterrence', *American Economic Review*, 69, 335–8.

Schmalensee, Richard (1978), 'Entry Deterrence in the Ready-to-Eat Breakfast Cereal Industry', *Bell Journal of Economics*, 9, 305–27.

Schwartz, M. (1986), 'The Nature and Scope of Contestability Theory', in Morris, D. J., Sinclair, P. J., Slater, M. D., and Vickers, J. S., eds., *Strategic Behaviour and Industrial Competition*, Oxford, Oxford University Press.

Spence, A. Michael (1977), 'Entry, Capacity, Investment and Oligopolistic Pricing', *Bell Journal of Economics*, 8, 534–44.

Stigler, G. J. (1968), *The Organization of Industry*, Homewood, Illinois, Richard D. Irwin.

Stiglitz, Joseph E. (1981), 'Potential Competition May Reduce Welfare', *American Economic Review*, 71, 184–9.

Stiglitz, Joseph E. (1987), 'Technological Change, Sunk Costs and Competition', *Brookings Papers on Economic Activity*, 3, 883–937.

Sylos-Labini, P. (1962), *Oligopoly and Technical Progress*, Cambridge, Harvard University Press.

Urban, G., Carter, T., Gaskin, S., and Mucha, Z. (1984), 'Market Share Reward to Pioneering Brands', *Management Science*, 32, 645–59.

US Department of Transportation (1988), *Study of Airline Computer Reservation Systems*, May.

West, Douglas S. (1981), 'Testing for Market Pre-emption Using Sequential Location Data', *Bell Journal of Economics*, Spring, 12, 129–43.

Weitzman, Martin L. (1983), 'Contestable Markets: An Uprising in the Theory of Industry Structure: Comment', *American Economic Review*, 73, 486–7.

Weizsäcker, Carl Christian von (1980), 'A Welfare Analysis of Barriers to Entry', *Bell Journal of Economics*, 11, 399–420.

Yip, G. S. (1982), *Barriers to Entry: A Corporate Strategy Perspective*, Lexington, Ballinger.

4

The Stability of Collusive Agreements: Some Recent Theoretical Developments

Jean Jaskold Gabszewicz

1. Introduction

Collusion between economic agents is an important ingredient in the organization of markets. Collusive agreements can have multiple objects—prices, production quotas, power delegation—and assume various institutional forms—cartels, mergers, syndicates, trade associations or unions, Central Industry Sales Bureaux. It has long been recognized that such agreements suffer from recurrent instability, and many reasons for such instability have been identified. Among them are the differences in oligopolists' cost structures and the differentiation of their products, which can make difficult the definition of price differentials. Also, the dynamic evolution of the market must require periodical negotiations to adjust the terms of the agreement to this changing environment. Furthermore, firms' expectations about future demand may differ, and reaching an agreement may require mutual comparisons of probability judgements about the events which influence market conditions. Last, but not least, government regulations against express cartel agreements may compound the complexity of defining an agreement, since firms are then enforced to rely on tacit co-ordination devices. However, all these considerations take for granted the fact that collusion should always be beneficial to the participants, and that only external shocks could create difficulties in managing collusion.

Notwithstanding, there is a more fundamental issue in the analysis of collusion: is it, indeed, in the interest of the ecomomic agents to substitute a collective constraint to their individual freedom, and to maintain this substitution through time? Surprisingly enough, while entry phenomena have been extensively analysed by industrial economists, the theoretical analysis of collusive behaviour—which operates in the reverse direction to entry—has been a rather neglected topic. Perhaps this is due to the Chamberlinian view, according to which, if sellers are few in number and products are homogeneous, the oligopolists must fully recognize their interdependence and their mutual interest to escape from destructive price wars:

If each seller seeks his maximum profit rationally and intelligently, he will realize that when there are only two or a few sellers, his own move has a considerable effect upon his competitors, and that this makes it idle to suppose that they will accept without retaliation the losses he forces upon them. Since the result of a cut by any one is inevitably to decrease his own profits, no one will cut, and although the sellers are entirely independent, the equilibrium result is the same as though there were a monopolistic agreement between them (Chamberlin 1933: 48).

It is only recently—under the impetus of a game-theoretic approach to the problem—that economists have taken a renewed interest in the question of collusive stability. The purpose of the present chapter is to review some of the theoretical contributions which have been developed around this general theme.

In the first section we examine the question of stability of collusive agreements using the concept of *core*. This approach is well adapted to the analysis of situations where groups of economic agents 'combine' together and agree to delegate a single decision unit the task of representing their economic interests. Many instances of such binding agreements are observed in real-life situations; think, for example, of trade unions, syndicates of consumers, professional associations, etc. Von Neumann and Morgenstern had already perceived how this type of collusive behaviour could bias the collective choice mechanism:

The classical definitions of free competition all involve further postulates besides the greatness of that number. E.g., it is clear that, if certain great groups of participants—for any reason whatsoever—act together, then the great number of participants may not become effective; the decisive exchanges may take place directly between large 'coalitions' (such as trade unions, consumers' co-operatives . . .), and not between individuals, many in number, acting independently (1944: 98).

Stability analysis is conducted here by comparing the outcomes in the core with, and without, syndicate formation. In particular, syndicate formation leads to the exclusion of some coalitions which would have existed otherwise: namely, those coalitions which would include a *proper* subset of a syndicate (by definition, the syndicate enters only 'as a whole' into broader coalitions). The excluded coalitions are no longer available to 'block' some collective outcomes, so that syndicate formation may widen the core to such outcomes. The question is whether these outcomes can be of benefit to syndicate members when compared with the outcomes obtained in the core without the existence of syndicates.

The second section is devoted to the study of a two-member price-setting cartel, examined from the viewpoint of non-co-operative theory. Consider an industry consisting of two firms selling a homogeneous product to a population of consumers. If they act without co-ordinating their price decisions, the competitive outcome (price = marginal cost) should most probably be expected. Indeed, if any one of them sets a price exceeding marginal cost, the other one can undercut it, and attract the whole demand into his business. The first seller is then expected to retaliate with a still lower price, and cut throat competition should drive down the price to marginal cost. It is precisely because Chamberlinian duopolists both anticipate this competition, that they are supposed to maintain, by tacit agreement, the monopoly price; then they form a price-setting cartel, and both firms find an advantage in the existence of the cartel. As a first approximation, the existence of co-operating forces for securing the monopoly price must accordingly be recognized. But divisive forces exist as well, for the very act of agreeing upon the monopoly price creates incentives for both sellers to expand output beyond the quotas which sustain this price, simply because at these quotas marginal receipt exceeds marginal cost. Accordingly, the price-setting cartel is not immune against individual cheatings and the stability of the arrangement depends on whether there are countervailing forces which act for preventing cartel members from effectively breaking its rules. In section 2, this situation is depicted as a non-co-operative game, the strategies of which are: 'observe the quota-cheat', and the conclusion of the stability analysis is rather negative in this set-up.

The next section considers again a price-setting cartel resulting from the collusion of n firms in a particular industry. Assuming that the cartel cannot put up a resistance to advantageous price cuts by some of its members, we study the remaining fragments of this cartel after it breaks down as a result of this 'chiselling'. The crucial assumption which is made here is that firms leaving the cartel have limited capacity so that, in any case, they can only serve a small part of market demand. Accordingly, an industrial structure could emerge in which the 'loyal' firms remaining in the original cartel still keep the monopoly price, simply because the free-riders, even using a lower price, can only supply a rather small share of the market. This structure is called a 'quasi-monopoly'. Some properties of a quasi-monopoly, and the stability of this market arrangement, are studied in section 3.

In sections 4 and 5, we adopt another approach, relying on the notion of 'coalition structure'. A coalition structure is a partition of the set of agents into a cartel and firms acting individually. The agents are assumed to choose independently the elements of the partition they decide to belong to. If k among n firms decide to belong to the cartel, the coalition structure consists of $1 + n - k$ elements: one cartel including k firms and $n - k$ firms acting individually as 'singletons'. To each coalition structure corresponds a vector of pay-offs to the firms resulting from the market solution which is supposed to realize, once the firms have decided whether or not to belong to the cartel. In section 4, we suppose that the market solution is the collusive-price-leadership outcome, in which the cartel including k firms sets a price which is accepted by the 'competitive fringe' consisting of the $n - k$ firms which have chosen to act individually. In section 5, the market solution is assumed to be a Cournot equilibrium of the non-co-operative game played by the cartel of k firms and the $n - k$ firms acting independently. In both cases, the stability of a particular coalition structure is studied by comparing the level of profits realized at the corresponding market solution by the insiders of the cartel to the level of profits they would have obtained if they had decided to remain outside the collusive agreement, or if this agreement had failed to realize its objective.

2.   Collusive Agreements and the Core

A major progress in the understanding of competitive market mechanisms in large economies has resulted from the analysis of the *core* of the market in the framework of pure exchange models (see e.g. Debreu and Scarf 1963, Aumann 1964, Hildenbrand 1974). The main conclusion of these studies is that when the number of traders becomes very large, the core tends to coincide with the set of competitive allocations. Using a simple illustration, I would like to examine in this section how the conclusions of this analysis should be amended when collusive phenomena take place in the similar context of a large economy.

To this end, I shall consider the following example of a productive economy using two factors of production Z_1 and Z_2—say, labour and capital—for producing some commodity 'via' the Cobb-Douglas production F defined by

$$F(Z_1, Z_2) = Z_1^{\frac{1}{2}} Z_2^{\frac{1}{2}}.$$

Assume that factors ownership is initially spread over n labourers (factor 1) each owning $\frac{1}{n}$ units of labour, and n capitalists (factor 2), each owning $\frac{1}{n}$ units of capital. A single unit of the product can be produced in this economy, and we are interested in the *imputations* of this unit among the factor owners, i.e. we are interested in vectors $x = (x_{11}, \cdots, x_{1j}, \cdots, x_{1n}; x_{21}, \cdots, x_{2j}, \cdots, x_{2n})$ verifying $\Sigma_{j=1}^{n} \times_{1j} + \Sigma_{j=1}^{n} \times_{2j} = 1$: an imputation is simply a distribution of the unit of product among the factor owners. In particular, the *competitive imputation* x^* assigns to each factor owner his marginal product, i.e.

$$x_{ij}^* = \frac{1}{n}\frac{\partial F}{\partial Z_i}\bigg|_{(1,1)} = \frac{1}{2n}, \qquad i = 1, 2;$$

(since F is constant returns to scale, Euler's theorem implies

$$N\left(\frac{1}{n}\frac{\partial F}{\partial Z_1}\bigg|_{(1,1)} + \frac{1}{n}\frac{\partial F}{\partial Z_2}\bigg|_{(1,1)}\right) = 1, \text{ and } x^* \text{ is an imputation).}$$

Define a *coalition* as a subset S of factor owners. Given a particular imputation x, no coalition S would accept this imputation if it can produce more of the product, on its own resources of factors, than the quantity assigned by this imputation to the members of the coalition S. Then the coalition S is said to *block* the proposed imputation. In other words, denoting by $|S_1|$ (resp. $|S_2|$) the number of labourers (resp. capitalists) who are members of S, the coalition *blocks* an imputation $x = (x_{11}, \cdots, x_{1n}; x_{21}, \cdots x_{2n})$ whenever

$$F(|S_1|, |S_2|) = |S_1|^{\frac{1}{2}} \cdot |S_2|^{\frac{1}{2}} > \sum_{1j \in S} x_{1j} + \sum_{2j \in S} x_{2j}.$$

By definition, the *core* is the set of all imputations which are not blocked by any coalition. If an imputation is in the core, no coalition can augment the quantity of product it receives under that imputation by producing independently from the factor owners who are not members of that coalition. It is well known that, *when the number* n *of factor owners of each type becomes large, the core tends to the sole competitive imputation* x* (for a formal proof see Hansen and Gabszewicz 1971). This is the analogue, for this production model, of the conclusion referred to above, for pure exchange economies.

Now, assume that all capitalists collude, and decide to form a syndicate. What is the effect on the core of this collusion process? Clearly the core cannot remain invariant under this collective decision: all coalitions including a *proper* subset of the capitalists are henceforth forbidden, since all capitalists act in unison. Consequently, the core must be redefined with respect to this new, restricted class of potential blocking coalitions. Since they are less numerous, more imputations can remain unblocked, so that the core is widened, and now includes all those imputations which would have been otherwise blocked by a coalition including a proper subset of capitalists. If syndicate formation has to be effective and stable, it should bring about in the core new imputations which guarantee to its members higher pay-offs than those obtained without syndicate formation: the individual members always remain free to break the agreement which binds them to the syndicate. For large values of n and in the absence of the syndicate, the core consists only of the competitive imputation x^*, assigning $\frac{1}{2n}$ to each factor owner. Accordingly, to guarantee the effectiveness and the stability of the syndicate, the core must now include at least some imputation x which assigns to syndicate members an amount of product exceeding $\frac{1}{2n}$. In fact, as we now show it, *the imputation x assigning $\frac{1}{n}$ to each capitalist in the syndicate, and 0 to each labourer is in the core when the syndicate of capitalists has been formed.* First, it is clear that the imputation $\underline{x}$ is Pareto optimal since it distributes the total amount which can be produced. Accordingly, if contrary to the above statement, the imputation x would not be in the core, the blocking coalition S cannot include all factor owners. It cannot be either a subset or the set of labourers, because the labourers can produce nothing without the help of capitalists. Consequently, if x is not in the core, it is blocked by a coalition S consisting of the syndicate of capitalists and a *proper* subset of labourers. Let v be the number of labourers in S, $v < n$. Since S blocks, we must have

$$\sum_{1j\epsilon S} x_{1j} + \sum_{2j\epsilon S} x_{2j} < F(|S_1|, |S_2|) = \left(\tfrac{v}{n}\right)^{\frac{1}{2}} \cdot \left(\tfrac{v}{n}\right)^{\frac{1}{2}} < 1, \qquad (1)$$

where the last inequality follows from the fact that $v < n$. However

$$\sum_{1j\epsilon S} x_{1j} + \sum_{2j\epsilon S} x_{2j} = \sum_{2j\epsilon S} x_{2j} = 1,$$

which contradicts the inequality (1): the imputation x is in the core. The intuitive reason for this result is that, combining together, the capitalists have made ineffective any coalition which does not include all of them in view of producing a strictly positive amount of the product: now they benefit from a 'veto power' on production, while before syndicate formation, coalitions gathering a subset of labourers and a proper subset of capitalists would have blocked an imputation like x. The mechanism underlying the above proposition is very similar to the following apology. A lady comes down from a train and three porters propose their services to carry her trunk from the train to a cab. One porter—say porter A—is not hefty enough to carry her trunk alone, but can succeed in doing it with the help of any one of the two other porters B or B'. On the other hand, porters B and B' are not strong enough to carry the trunk together (and, *a fortiori*, alone). The lady is offering a 100 francs reward for the carriage of the trunk. How will the porters share this amount among them? A simple reasoning shows that the only possible outcome in the core consists in assigning the total amount to porter A; otherwise, indeed, a coalition can form between porter A and any one of the two other porters, in view of carrying the trunk together and sharing among them the amount that the remaining porter would have obtained. This prevents any outcome in which either porter B or B' would receive a strictly positive amount of the reward.

Interestingly enough, other propositions can be demonstrated concerning the stability of syndicate formation in a framework analogous to the one considered here. In particular, it can be shown that if no syndicate includes *all* the owners of one factor, those factor owners who are not syndicate members necessarily get in the core the competitive pay-off (for large values of n).

Accordingly, either *all* factor owners get their marginal product—in which case the syndicates are ineffective—or the syndicates necessarily 'take from each other'. In the latter case, one should not expect the syndicate structure to be stable, since those syndicate members which receive less than their marginal product can always obtain it by leaving their syndicate. Thus it is only in the extreme case described above—with a syndicate monopolizing the total amount of a factor—that a syndicate structure must be expected to achieve stability.[1]

3. A 'Prisoner's Dilemma': The Price-Setting Cartel

Let us come back to the analysis of the two firms' price-setting cartel considered in our introduction. We have seen that if the two firms succeed in forming a cartel they obtain higher joint profits than those they would realize under the competitive conditions. In particular, they can quote the monopoly price, and share the monopoly profits among them. Then they lie on the Pareto-surface, where the profits of the firms cannot be simultaneously increased as on Figure 4.1 at point q.

Let x_i^q, $i = 1,2$ denote the quota of firm i corresponding to the monopoly output, and $I_i^1, \cdots, I_i^4$ the isoprofits curve of member i, with the profits along I_i^1 greater than the profits along I_i^2, a.s.o. Assuming that firm j will observe the quota x_j^q, firm i would increase its profits if it cheats and expands production to x_i^c. Accordingly, each firm is better off cheating when it assumes that its opponent will keep observing the quota. On the other hand, Figure 4.1 reveals that, when it assumes that its opponent cheats, each firm is also better off cheating: for instance, assuming firm 2 cheats and chooses x_2^c, cheating and choosing x_1^c leads firm 1 on a higher isoprofits curve (I_1^1) than the isoprofits curve (I_1^4) reached when sticking to the quota x_1^q. Accordingly, in any circumstances—whether its opponent cheats or observes the quota—each firm is better off cheating than observing the quota! Osborne (1976) has represented this situation in the formal set-up of non-co-operative

---

[1] The interested reader is referred to Hansen and Gabszewicz 1971 for further details on this analysis; also the counterpart of these developments for the case of pure exchange economies can be found in Gabszewicz and Drèze 1971, and Postlewaite and Roberts 1977.

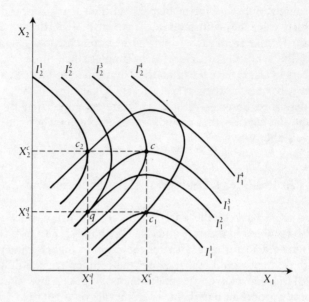

Fig. 4.1 The Price-Setting Cartel

game theory. Each cartel member is assumed to be the player of a
two-person non-co-operative game, having at his disposal two
possible strategies: 'observe the quota or cheat', and as pay-offs in
the pay-off matrix, the profits obtained at points q, c, c_1 and c_2 in
Figure 4.1. The pay-off matrix in Figure 4.2 satisfies the profits
relationship observed at these points, namely that, whether the
outcome is in column 1 or 2, member 1 prefers to cheat; and
whether the outcome is in row 1 or 2, member 2 prefers to cheat. It
has the property of a 'Prisoner's Dilemma' game: any co-operative
outcome can be reached only if at least one of the two players plays
a dominated strategy (for instance, if player 1 observes the quota,
the outcome (4,4) can obtain only if player 2 also chooses the

	Observe	Cheat
Observe	4,4	1,5
Cheat	5,1	3,3

Fig. 4.2 Pay-off Matrix

strategy 'observe the quota', a strategy which is dominated by the strategy 'cheat'. The conclusion is that, without having recourse to some external device to resolve the dilemma (like an enforceable contract), the price-setting cartel must be expected to collapse.

This conclusion should, however, be amended if one takes into account the *repeated* structure of the game played by the cartel members. Consider the infinitely repeated 'Prisoner's Dilemma' game, where after each stage, each player observes the action of the other player (see Aumann 1985). The so-called 'Folk theorem' guarantees that any pair of infinitely repeated individually rational pay-offs of the one-shot game constitute a *non-co-operative* equilibrium pair of pay-offs in the supergame. In particular, the pair of strategies where players always repeat the co-operative play (observe-observe) is a non-co-operative equilibrium pair of strategies in the repeated game. The intuitive reason for this result is that if one player would deviate from it at some stage of the repeated game, his opponent can punish him by using for ever the non-co-operative strategy of the one-shot game; the potential use of this threat makes disadvantageous the initial deviation from the co-operative strategy. Accordingly, co-operation is achieved through the repeated nature of the game, even if it is played non-co-operatively. This is exactly, in game-theoretic terms, the argument underlying the Chamberlinian line of reasoning to explain tacit agreements in duopoly. One must insist, however, that this line of reasoning is valid only when the game is *infinitely* repeated; otherwise, and for *any* finite horizon game, we are led back to the conclusion that the cartel is unstable. Suppose indeed that the game defined by the above pay-off matrix is repeated a finite number of times only, say for T periods. To get the intuition for that result, let us consider the following backward-induction argument. Clearly, at period T, both players will choose the strategy 'cheat': no unilateral move from this pair can be advantageous at that period since the game is terminated afterwards. Knowing that both will choose the non-co-operative strategy at period T, it is also optimal for both players to choose the same strategy at period $T - 1$. Proceeding recursively, it is finally optimal to play non-co-operatively in all periods! Accordingly, the only non-co-operative equilibrium pair of strategies in the finite horizon game consists in repeating the non-co-operative pair of strategies of the one-shot game.

4. Cartel's Stability and Capacity Constraints

In the previous section we have concluded that, except if the cartel game is infinitely repeated or if an enforceable contract is signed by its members, a price-setting cartel must be expected to collapse, and the non-co-operative outcome should be observed. As we shall see in the present section, it may be, however, that *capacity constraints* can induce firms in an industry to remain close to the co-operative agreement, in spite of the arguments developed in the preceding section, where no such constraints have been imposed. Consider an industry embodying *n* enterprises which have initially agreed to combine and form a cartel. As illustrated above, one should expect some firms to cheat and expand output beyond the quantity which sustains the monopoly price. Assume, however, that the 'chisellers' incur capacity constraints, so that they cannot serve the whole demand which their manœuvre has attracted. Which market structure should be expected as a result of these combined pressures? Our contention is that after the cartel has broken down, a new market structure may emerge, which remains close, but not identical, to the starting collusive arrangement. We call this structure a 'quasi-monopoly'.

To illustrate the concept, consider the following story (D'Aspremont and Gabszewicz (1983: 143)).

Imagine a town full of taxis whose drivers are organized into a powerful cartel controlling the whole city. They have agreed to fix a rate per mile equal to, or approaching, the monopoly fare. Some of these taxi-drivers may be tempted to organize a conspiracy against the cartel and undercut the official fare: this will considerably expand the number of their customers, possibly in excess to the number of taxis available to the chisellers! The original cartel will then break down into two fragments. The first fragment groups all 'loyal' cartel members, the second, the chisellers. Of course, the temptation is great for the first group to retaliate, and in turn to quote a still lower price so as to recover its customers. But as a result of this price war the fare may descend to its competitive level, which could hurt them severely, presumably more severely than if they would stick to the original monopolistic fare. In fact, the extent to which the loyal members are hurt depends crucially on the number of chisellers. *If this number is small, the chisellers hit their capacity, and the residual demand would in any case be served by cartel members at the monopoly fare.* This suggests that the loyal cartel members might tolerate the erection of a 'splinter group' if the latter is sufficiently small—small enough, that is, to ensure that it is still advantageous to keep the monopoly price rather than enter a price war. The market structure presumably prevailing at the end will consist of two cartels of very unequal size: a small free-rider cartel quoting a price slightly below the monopoly price, and the cartel of 'loyal' taxi-drivers still demanding the monopoly price because it knows that its competitor can only supply a very small share of the market. As described above, the final structure is similar to the case of a single cartel quoting the monopoly price, i.e., a quasi-monopoly.

The notion of quasi-monopoly can be formally defined for an industry embodying n identical firms in the following manner. Let $D(p)$ be the market demand function, and assume that the capacity of each firm is exactly equal to $\frac{1}{n}$. Assume also that marginal cost is constant and, without loss of generality, normalize it at zero. Let p_M be the monopoly price, and suppose that joint profit maximization has successfully raised the price at the level p_M. Imagine now that, according to the mechanism described in the previous section, some cartel members—say, k firms among the n firms in the cartel— decide to break the agreement, and start to quote a price lower than p_M. Then the supply side of the market is made of *two* cartels, the cartel of 'loyal' firms—say, cartel α—embodying $n - k$ firms and with capacity equal to $\frac{n-k}{n} \overset{\text{def}}{=} \alpha$, and the cartel of deviant firms— say, cartel β −, embodying k firms with capacity equal to $\frac{k}{n} \overset{\text{def}}{=} \beta$, and quoting a lower price than p_M. Finally, denote by $\Pi_\alpha(p_\alpha, p_\beta)$ (resp. $\Pi_\beta(p_\alpha, p_\beta)$) the joint profits of firms in cartel α (resp. β) if cartel α (resp. β) quotes a price p_α (resp. p_β). We define a *quasi-monopoly* as a pair of prices $(p_M \, \bar{p}_\beta)$ where p_M is the monopoly price and $\bar{p}_\beta$ meets the following requirements:

$$\Pi_\beta(p_M, \bar{p}_\beta) > \Pi_\beta(p_M, p_M) \tag{3}$$

$$\Pi_\beta(p_M, \bar{p}_\beta) = \max_{p_\beta} \Pi_\beta(p_M, p_\beta) \tag{4}$$

for all p_β such that, $\forall p_\alpha, \Pi_\alpha(p_M, p_\beta) \geqslant \Pi_\alpha(p_\alpha, p_\beta)$.

The first condition guarantees that the cartel β of deviant firms have larger profits than their original share in the monopoly profits. The second condition ensures that, given p_M, the deviant firms maximize their joint profits at $\bar{p}_\beta$, but only in the range of p_β − values for which it remains optimal for the cartel α of loyal firms to keep the monopoly price p_M.

The emergence of a quasi-monopoly as a consequence of cartel instability rests on the following considerations. First of all, breaking the initial cartel agreement only makes sense if the chisellers gain higher profits after their exit from the cartel: hence, condition (3). Secondly, a price war should be avoided, and this is possible because the chisellers meet capacity constraints: indeed, the incentive to retaliate against a price cut is weakened because, in any case, the capacity of the deviant firms is so small that it deprives cartel α of only a small part of monopoly demand; maintaining monopoly price is more advantageous than entering a price war: hence condition (4). Finally, a non-co-operative price equilibrium in the game where cartels α and β are the players cannot be considered as an alternative solution to a quasi-monopoly: it can be shown, indeed, that in a duopoly where firms incur capacity constraints, a non-co-operative price equilibrium necessarily fails to exist.[2] Accordingly, even if the breakdown of the original cartel agreement gives rise to a duopoly with capacity constraints, the situation cannot stabilize afterwards at a non-co-operative solution; this reinforces indirectly the possible emergence of a quasi-monopoly.

In my paper with C. D'Aspremont (1983), it is shown that there always exists a size of the cartel β which is small enough to guarantee that a quasi-monopoly solution exists for this size of cartel β (Appendix, Proposition 2). Secondly, we show that no quasi-monopoly solution can exist if the group of deviant firms is not strictly smaller than $\frac{n}{2}$. This confirms the initial intuition that, with capacity constraints, the cartel of free riders must be small if it has to be effective. Finally, the stability of the quasi-monopoly arrangement is discussed: the question is whether a quasi-monopoly is not in turn a transitory arrangement. In fact, it can be shown that at a quasi-monopoly solution, deviant firms enjoy higher profits than the loyal firms. On the other hand, the profits of each deviant firm is a strictly decreasing function of the size of cartel β. Consequently, no firm in the splinter group would consider leaving the group and joining the 'loyalists'. Conversely, any firm in the loyal cartel would find it advantageous to join the group of deviant firms. However, this group is not willing to accept new members since it leads to the erosion of their profits. This rejection

---

[2] The argument for the non-existence of a price equilibrium in a duopoly with capacity constraints has been presented as early as 1925 by Edgeworth (1925).

of new memberships thus creates a countervailing effect to the tendency of the splinter group to grow indefinitely.

In the next section we come back to the multiple firms' cartel problem without capacity constraints, but adopt a very different approach relying on the notion of collusive price leadership.

5.   The Collusive Price Leadership Cartel

A possible objection against the analysis of section 2 is that the formation of cartels generally takes place in more complex industrial structures than the one considered there. In particular, more than two firms compose the industry, and it seems that the more firms a market includes, the more difficult is price co-ordination. When they are numerous, individual sellers are increasingly tempted to cheat, hoping that a deviation from their assigned quota will have no significant effect on aggregate output and overall level of price. Furthermore, the more they are, the more difficult to harmonize their conflicting views about the sharing of the profits. It has been observed in many industries that business practices tend to privilege a particular implicit mean for price co-ordination, avoiding thereby the dangers inherent to the existence of a large number of market participants. This practice consists in the recognition and acceptance by all firms of a *price leader*, which sets the price and imposes it to the fringe of competitors acting in the same industry. The dominant firm sets the price that best serves its own interest, taking into account the supply reactions of the fringe firms. The power of acting as a price leader is often evolved to a cartel consisting of a subset of firms which have succeeded in combining together, and act in unison when choosing price in view of maximizing the profit per firm in the cartel. Those firms which are not cartel members then remain in the 'competitive fringe', and accept the price set by the collusive price-leadership cartel. The analysis of pricing co-ordination via price leadership has been proposed by Markham (1951), and the stability of this collusive process has been examined by D'Aspremont, Gabszewicz, Jacquemin, and Weymark (1983).

Denote by $D(p)$ the demand to the industry as a function of the price p. Suppose that the industry is composed of n identical firms, each with total cost function $C(q)$ where q denotes the firm's output. Suppose also that a number k among these n firms collude, and succeed in becoming a price-leadership cartel; then $n - k$ firms remain in the competitive fringe. Since all these firms are assumed to accept the cartel's price p as given, each of them supplies that level of output, $S(p)$, for which marginal cost equals the price p. Accordingly, at price p, the competitive fringe supplies the market for an amount equal to $(n - k) \cdot S(p)$, so that the *residual demand* to be served by the cartel is equal to $RD(p,k) \stackrel{\text{def}}{=} D(p) - (n - k) \cdot S(p)$.

If, at each price, total profits of the cartel and total output to be produced are uniformly shared among the cartel members, the profit *per firm* in the cartel obtains as

$$\pi_d(p, k) \stackrel{\text{def}}{=} p \cdot \left[\frac{D(p) - (n - k) \cdot S(p)}{k} \right] - C \left(\left[\frac{D(p) - (n - k) \cdot S(p)}{k} \right] \right).$$

Maximizing π_d with respect to p leads to the optimal price $p^*(k)$ to be announced by a cartel including k firms and to a maximal per firm profit equal to $\pi_d(p^*(k),k)$. As for the $n - k$ firms in the competitive fringe, they obtain each a profit $\pi_c(p^*(k),k)$ defined by $\pi_c(p^*(k),k) = p^*(k) \cdot S(p^*(k)) - C(S(p^*(k)))$.

When may a price-leadership collusive agreement between k firms be regarded as stable? First, it must guarantee to cartel members higher profits than those realized under competitive conditions, when all firms act independently. It is readily verified that this condition is, indeed, realized, since the cartel behaves as a monopolist with respect to the residual demand curve $RD(p, k)$. On the other hand, stability requires that cartel members' profits dominate those profits they could obtain otherwise at the outcome which would be realized if they left the cartel: this is a condition of *internal* stability. Finally, one could also impose a condition of *external* stability: this would require that firms which are *not* cartel members obtain as high a profit when remaining outside the cartel as the one obtained when joining it. A move of a firm inside (resp. outside) a cartel including k members, leads to a new cartel including $k + 1$ (resp. $k - 1$) members; thus, internal stability of a k-member cartel is satisfied if, and only if,

$$\pi_d(p^*(k), k) \geq \pi_c(p^*(k - 1); k - 1):$$

the left-hand term of this inequality is the profit per firm obtained with a k-members' cartel, while the right-hand term is the profit a firm leaving the cartel with k members would obtain in the competitive fringe after its defection from the cartel.

Similarly, external stability of a k-members' cartel requires that

$$\pi_c(p^*(k), k) \geq \pi_d(p^*(k + 1), k + 1):$$

profit of a firm in the fringe is as high as the profits it would enjoy should it join the cartel. With an internally stable cartel there is no incentive for a cartel member to leave the cartel; with an externally stable cartel, there is no incentive for a fringe firm to join it.

It is interesting to point out the analogy between the notions of internal and external stability, and the notion of a subgame perfect Nash equilibrium of the following 2-stage game. At stage 1, each of the n firms has to choose whether to belong to a cartel, or to act independently. Then, at stage 2, the decisions of all firms are revealed and pay-offs to the 'players' are determined according to the above theory of price leadership, i.e. the cartel resulting from stage 1 chooses the optimal price on the corresponding residual demand, and firms who have decided to remain in the fringe accept this price. If a cartel of size k is both internally and externally stable, it is impossible that a firm could gain by deviating unilaterally from its choice at stage 1 (leaving the cartel or leaving the fringe) if the other firms stick to their own choice, and vice versa. Accordingly, a price-leadership cartel of k firms is internally and externally stable if, and only if, there exists a subgame perfect Nash equilibrium of the above 2-stage game at which exactly k firms decide to belong to a cartel.[3]

First notice that, for a fixed value of k, the profits of a firm outside the cartel are always larger than the profits of a firm inside the cartel. To prove this assertion, let us consider Figure 4.3 where R_M and R_m denote, respectively, the average and marginal revenues *per firm* in the cartel, as derived from the residual demand $RD(p,k)$. Since $p^*(k)$ maximizes the profits per firm in the cartel, each firm belonging to it must produce at q^*_D, where marginal cost MC equals marginal revenue R_m, so that profit per firm in the cartel is represented by the shaded area in Figure 4.3. A firm in the

[3] A 'strong-equilibrium' notion, for which no *subgroup* of firms could find an advantageous unilateral move, could also be defined. This approach is adopted by Hart and Kurz (1985) in the context of an extension of the Shapley value.

competitive fringe accepts the price $p^*(k)$ and maximizes its profits at q^*_c where marginal cost MC is equal to $p^*(k)$. Accordingly, the profits of a firm in the fringe not only include the shaded area but also the area ABC, which proves the above assertion.

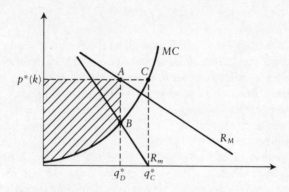

Fig. 4.3 The Profit of a Cartel Member is Lower than the Profit of a Firm in the Competitive Fringe

Notice also that a cartel including k firms is internally stable if, and only if, the cartel including $k - 1$ firms is externally stable. This remark allows us to prove that it is always possible to find a group of firms that can form a collusive cartel which is both internally and externally stable. The proof proceeds as follows. Clearly the profits of a cartel consisting of a single firm are higher than the profits this firm would obtain if there were no cartel at all and if all the n firms would act competitively: the single firm's cartel benefits by taking into account the discrepancy between marginal and average revenues corresponding to the residual demand $RD(p,1)$. Thus, the cartel with $k = 1$ is internally stable. If it is also externally stable, then the assertion is proved since we would have found a cartel which is both internally and externally stable. If the cartel with $k = 1$ is not externally stable, then, by the above remark, the cartel with $k = 2$ is internally stable and, if it is also externally stable, the assertion is proved. Continuing in this manner, either a cartel which is both internally and externally stable is found for $k < n$; or, for $k = n$, we obtain a cartel which is internally stable. Since in that case there are no further firms to join the cartel, the cartel with $k = n$ (the monopoly cartel) is also externally stable, which completes the proof of the above assertion.

Consequently, to the extent that individual firms take into account in evaluating their profits the impact of their own entry or exit from a dominant cartel, there always exists a collusive price-leadership cartel which satisfies the two criteria of stability. Then if the size of the stable cartel approaches the total number of firms in the industry, the market price will also approach the monopoly price, and would coincide with it if all firms are members of the stable cartel.

A particular example of the above analysis is studied in D'Aspremont and Gabszewicz 1985. The industry is assumed to be composed of five firms, with total cost function $C(q)$ defined by

$$C(q) = \frac{q^2}{2}.$$

Industry demand is assumed to be given by

$$D(p) = 5(1-p).$$

Then it is easy to derive the explicit analytical forms of $p^*(k)$, $\pi_d(p^*(k), k)$ and $\pi_c(p^*(k), k)$, $k = 1, \cdots, 5$, i.e.

$$p^*(k) = \frac{2}{(4 - \frac{k}{5})^2};$$
$$\pi_d(p^*(k), k) = \frac{1}{2(4 - \frac{k}{5})^2};$$
$$\pi_c(p^*(k), k) = \frac{2}{[4 - (\frac{k}{5})^2]^2}.$$

Table 4.1 provides the values of π_d and π_c for $k = 1, \cdots, 5$. From direct comparison of profits we find out that the only cartel which is both internally and externally stable includes exactly 3 firms ($k = 3$).

k	0	1	2	3	4	5
π_d	—	0.126	0.130	0.137	0.149	0.161
π_c	0.125	0.128	0.136	0.151	0.177	—

Elaborating on an extension of this example, Donsimoni, Economides, and Polemarchakis (1986) have shown that, if firms are not 'too cost efficient' relative to market demand, there exists only one cartel which is both internally and externally stable. Otherwise, there exist industry sizes (values of n) for which two cartels are stable, one of which comprises all firms in the industry (monopoly cartel). They also show, for the same extension, that the relative size of stable cartels is a decreasing function of the size of the market.[4]

The preceding analysis of collusion is of course particular, to the extent that it refers to a particular market arrangement: the collusive-price-leadership solution. But similar analyses can be carried out for alternative solution concepts. In the same vein, Salant, Switzer, and Reynolds (1983) have studied the consequences of a merger on the Cournot outcome of a particular industry. The next section is devoted to a brief presentation of this contribution.

6.   Mergers and Cournot Oligopoly

Classical oligopoly theory assumes that firms in the industry choose independently their output level, given the outputs of the other firms. All firms are conscious that the level of the industry price not only depends on their own output decision, but also on their rivals' supply. Accordingly, if firms do not co-operate, equilibrium in the industry requires that no incentive—like an unexploited increase in profits—exists for a firm to deviate from its individual output choice, given the supply of its competitors. This leads to the concept of *Cournot equilibrium*, which is defined as a collection of output levels—one per firm—such that no firm can increase its profits if it deviates unilaterally from its choice, given the output levels chosen by the other firms.

To illustrate, we have depicted in Figure 4.4 the Cournot equilibrium in an industry embodying two firms acting as rival duopolists; q_1 and q_2 denote the output of firms 1 and 2, respectively.

---

[4] In a recent work, Rothschild (1988) analyses the case in which deviation from the dominant group to the competitive fringe is deterred by the prospect that other firms would find it in their interest to follow.

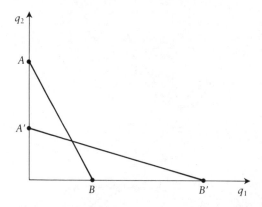

Fig. 4.4 The Reaction Functions of the Duopolists

The line AB (resp. $A'B'$) represents the locus of output levels of the firms for which firm 1's output (resp. firm 2) maximizes the profit of firm 1 (resp. firm 2), given the corresponding supply of firm 2 (resp. firm 1). These lines are called the *reaction functions* of the firms: they provide, for each output level of its competitor, the corresponding profit-maximizing output of the firm. Since a Cournot equilibrium requires that both firms maximize their profits against the output choice of their competitor, this equilibrium lies at the intersection of the reaction functions, i.e. at point C.

Now, let us come back to the n firms' industry case and suppose that a subset of k firms among them decide to *merge*, substituting to individual decision-making the unified control of the merged entity. Then, individual firms participating to the merger agreement become a collection of k plants, the total output of which constitutes the market supply of the merger. This changes the industry structure since there remain only $(n - k) + 1$ 'players' in the Cournot game after the merger agreement: $(n - k)$ of them continue to behave independently, while k of them act in unison. It is convenient to refer to the former as the 'outsiders', and to the latter as the 'insiders'. The first question to be raised about the 'stability' of such a merger agreement, is whether it would guarantee to the participants a higher profit than the pay-off which occurs to them, should the merger fail to succeed. Assuming that a Cournot equilibrium obtains when all firms operate independently,

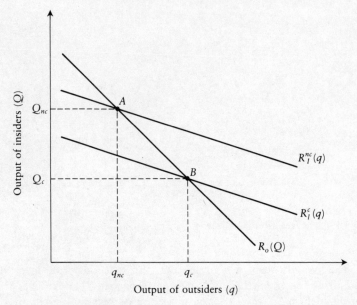

Fig. 4.5 The Pre-Merger (A) and Post-Merger (B) Equilibria

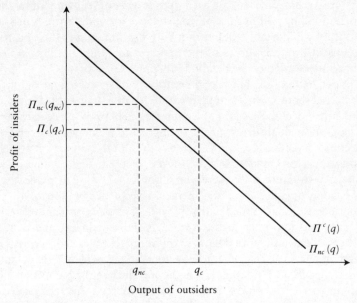

Fig. 4.6 The Pre-Merger and Post-Merger Total Profits of the Insiders

this amounts to comparing the pay-offs of the participating firms at this Cournot equilibrium with the pay-offs they would obtain as insiders of the merger, i.e. at the Cournot equilibrium in which the subset of k insiders merge while the other $(n - k)$ outsiders remain independent. Surprisingly enough, Salant *et al.* (1983) have shown that there exist exogenous mergers which reduce the endogenous joint profits of the firms that are assumed to collude.

To give an insight into the possibility of 'potential loss from horizontal merger', it is useful to refer to Figures 4.5 and 4.6.

Denote by $R_o(Q)$ in Figure 4.5 the reaction function of the outsiders for any given aggregate production Q by insiders ($R_o(Q)$ can easily be computed by deducting Q from the demand function, computing the Cournot equilibrium among the outsiders relative to this residual demand, and adding up the resulting output of each outsider firm). Denote by $R_I^{nc}(q)$ the total amount that the insiders would produce *prior to merger* for any given aggregate output q of outsiders ($R_I^{nc}(q)$ can easily be computed by deducting q from the demand function, computing the Cournot equilibrium among the insiders relative to this residual demand, and adding up the resulting output of each insider firm). $R_I^{nc}(q)$ is the reaction function of the insiders, *should they act independently*, for any given aggregate production q by outsiders. Accordingly, the total amounts produced at the *pre-merger* Cournot equilibrium, by outsiders and insiders, are given, respectively, by the horizontal and vertical components of point A in Figure 4.5. An exogenous merger will displace the equilibrium from A to B. To see this, consider the new reaction function $R_I^s(q)$ of the insiders *after they have merged*. It lies below the pre-merger reaction function, since for any output Q of the outsiders they now supply a smaller amount of output than before. This is so because joint profit maximization of insiders leads them to contract output as they internalize the losses that they were imparting to each other when competing individually. Since the best reply of outsiders to insiders' production does not depend on whether insiders act as a merger entity or as individual firms, their post- and pre-merger reaction functions coincide. Accordingly, the intersection of $R_I^c(q)$ and $R_o(Q)$ now lies at point B, which is the post-merger Cournot equilibrium. Hence the displacement of equilibrium entails a contraction of insiders' output and an expansion of outsiders' output. The net effect of these moves on insiders' profits has still to be examined.

To this end consider Figure 4.6 where the pre-merger and post-merger total profits of the insiders are depicted as a function of the output of outsiders, i.e. $\pi^{nc}(q)$ and $\pi^c(q)$, respectively. For any supply of the outsiders, insiders' total profits can only increase as a consequence of the merger move (they can always run their plants so as to 'mimic' the pre-merger output): this is why $\pi^c(q)$ lies above $\pi^{nc}(q)$. But as total output of the outsiders increases, the profits of the insiders decrease. Therefore, the possibility exists that the output expansion of the outsiders' firms resulting from the merger move finally reduces insider profits by more than the increase in their profits, had outsider production remained constant. This possibility is illustrated on Figure 4.6, where the merger move entails an outsider increase in production equal to $(q_c - q_{nc})$.

Using a linear demand function and assuming n identical firms with constant marginal cost, Salant *et al.* (1983) have shown that this loss resulting from horizontal merger can be observed in this particular context. More than that: in that case no merger can be beneficial to its members, should less than 50 per cent of the firms collude! Hence, contrary to a price-leadership agreement which was always beneficial to the colluding firms, a merger agreement can cause prejudice to its participants. Then, the very basic condition for the stability of collusion is violated.

Interesting questions are still to be answered in the framework proposed by Salant *et al.* (1983). Among them we note: Are there situations where the *only* profitable merger would be the merger to monopoly? Does there exist, among the set of profitable mergers, at least one merger which is both internally and externally stable? This seems to be a fruitful area for further research.

7.   Conclusion

In this chapter we have presented some recent developments in the analysis of collusive behaviour between economic agents. This is clearly a transitory report, since research in the field is developing rapidly in various directions. We have chosen in favour of a *theoretical* approach to the study of collusion's stability and we have voluntarily left aside many factual elements which can drastically affect this stability. Among these elements are the specific social structure of a particular industry, the differences between the technologies of the firms and the heterogeneity of the products they sell.

In our analysis of stability, we have concentrated on a method inspired from comparative static analysis, treating a collusive agreement between firms as an exogenous change in market structure that displaces the initial 'equilibrium set' of outcomes: the price-leadership outcome, the Cournot equilibrium, or the core of the market. A basic requirement for stability is that the pay-offs to the colluding agents are increased at the 'new' equilibria. More stringent conditions of stability can be imposed, like internal stability (whereby no colluding agent would gain by breaking the agreement), or external stability (whereby no colluding agent wishes to join the agreement). The next natural methodological step for developing the theory would be to treat the decision of collusion as a move of firms in an enlarged game, so as to endogenize this decision, rather than simply comparing the '*ex ante*' equilibria with the '*ex post*' ones. A first step in this direction has been proposed by Salant *et al.* (1983). But much remains to be done in what looks like a promising research territory.

References

Aumann, R. (1964), 'Markets with a Continuum of Traders', *Econometrica*, 32: 39–50.

—— (1973), 'Disadvantageous Monopolies', *Journal of Economc Theory*, 6: 1–11.

—— (1985), 'Repeated Games', in G. Feiwel (ed.), *Issues in Contemporary Microeconomics*, Macmillan, London.

D'Aspremont, C., Jacquemin, A., Gabszewicz, J. J., and Weymark, J. (1983), 'On the Stability of Collusive Price Leadership', *Canadian Journal of Economics*, 14: 17–25.

D'Aspremont, C. and Gabszewicz, J. J. (1983), 'Quasi-Monopolies', *Economica*, 52: 141–51.

—— and —— (1985), 'On the Stability of Collusion', in Stiglitz Joseph E. and G. Frank Mathewson (eds.), *New Developments in the Analysis of Market Structure*, MIT Press, New York.

Chamberlin, E. H. (1933), *The Theory of Monopolistic Competition*, Harvard University Press, Cambridge, Mass.

Debreu, G. and Scarf, H. (1963), 'A Limit Theorem on the Core of an Economy', *International Economic Review*, 4: 235–46.

Donsimoni, M., Economides, N., and Polemarchakis, H. (1986), 'Stable Cartels', *International Economic Review*, 27: 317–27.

Edgeworth, F. Y. (1925), *Papers Relating to Political Economy*, vol. 1, Macmillan, London.

Gabszewicz, J. J. and Drèze, J. H. (1971), 'Syndicates of Traders in an Exchange Economy', in H. W. Kuhn and G. Szegö (eds.), *Differential Games and Related Topics*, North-Holland, Amsterdam, 399–414.

Hansen, T. and Gabszewicz, J. J. (1971), 'Collusion of Factor Owners and Distribution of Social Output', *Journal of Economic Theory*, 4: 1–8.

Hart, S. and Kurz, M. (1983), 'Endogenous Formation of Coalitions', *Econometrica*, 51: 1047–64.

Hildenbrand, W. (1974), *Core and Equilibria of a Large Economy*, Princeton University Press, Princeton, N. J.

Markham, J. W. (1951), 'The Nature and Significance of Price-Leadership', *American Economic Review*, 41: 891–905.

Osborne, D. K. (1976), 'Cartel Problems', *American Economic Review*, 66: 835–44.

Postlewaite, A. and Roberts, J. D. (1977), 'A Note on the Stability of Large Cartels', *Econometrica*, 45: 1877–8.

Rothschild, R. (1988), 'The Stability of Dominant-Group Cartel', mimeo, Market Structures and Strategy Conference, University of Dundee.

Salant, J. W., Switzer, J., and Reynolds, R. (1983), 'Losses from Horizontal Merger: The Effects of an Exogenous Change in Industry Structure on Cournot-Nash Equilibrium', *Quarterly Journal of Economics*, 98: 185–9.

Von Neumann, J. and Morgenstern, O. (1944), *Theory of Games and Economic Behaviour*, Princeton University Press, Princeton, N. J.

5

Competition-Reducing Vertical Restraints

Jean Tirole

1. Introduction

Much economic activity involves delegation to agents. Wholesalers and retailers distribute a manufacturer's products. A defence contractor or an electric utility procures goods for government or regulatory agencies. An employee performs specified tasks for an employer. These three examples differ in many respects, but they have one common feature: they involve a small number of parties (often one) on each side of the 'market'. It is therefore unlikely that the traditional precepts of competitive equilibrium analysis (including optimality of linear pricing) apply to such transactions. More complex contracts than the specification of a transfer proportional to the quantity exchanged are called for.

This selective (and, therefore, incomplete) survey focuses on vertical control of retailers (or wholesalers), although, as we will see, some of the conclusions carry over to other vertical relationships. Retailing offers many instances of non-linear pricing or, more generally, 'vertical restraints'. In addition to the wholesale price (which forms the basis for a transfer linear in the quantity supplied to the retailer), the manufacturer may impose a franchise fee (a lump-sum to be paid by the retailer, independent of the size of the transaction); resale price maintenance (RPM, fixing the consumer price); exclusive territories (assigning the retailer a monopoly in distribution over some market segment); exclusive dealing (prohibiting the retailer from distributing goods from other manufacturers); a tie-in (that forces the retailer to buy an array of goods, rather than a single good, from the manufacturer); a long-term contract or penalties for breach; a transfer of residual rights of control to the manufacturer through vertical integration; etc. This wide variety of instruments suggests a need for a sophisticated analysis of vertical control.

Optimal business strategy is not the only stake of the analysis. The small-number situation and the widespread departure from linear pricing suggest that the welfare properties of competitive equilibrium may not hold; that is, arrangements that are privately optimal may not be socially desirable. This issue is of considerable importance for policy analysis. Most countries' antitrust laws or regulations restrict the use of some of these vertical restraints. For instance, in the United States, RPM and tie-ins are in principle illegal (tie-ins are actually often subject to the rule of reason); by contrast, exclusive dealing and exclusive territories may be prohibited depending on the circumstances. Franchise fees are legal *per se*. The economic analysis underlying such rules is admittedly weak; and they have generated, and still generate, considerable controversy. The issue is whether vertical restraints are motivated by pure efficiency reasons or whether they help the vertical structure to exercise monopoly power. The efficient (cost-minimizing) organization of a vertical structure is a desirable activity, and society can only approve of vertical restraints that are used for this purpose. By contrast, vertical restraints that exert negative externalities on third parties (consumers, other firms) should be scrutinized more thoroughly.

This paper surveys the role of vertical restraints in reducing competition between agents (e.g., retailers). Before doing so, we should remind the reader of some classic aspects of the *bilateral monopoly* relationship (single manufacturer–single retailer).[1] Suppose that the manufacturer uses linear pricing to sell his product to the retailer. Let p_w denote the wholesale price and c the manufacturer's unit production cost (which we assume is constant for simplicity). The manufacturer makes a profit only if $p_w > c$. And indeed he optimally exercises his monopoly power by charging a wholesale price exceeding his unit cost. This creates a vertical externality between the manufacturer and the retailer. Suppose that the retailers take actions that affect the demand for the good produced by the manufacturer. Then, every time the retailer increases demand for his good by one unit, the manufacturer's profit is increased by $p_w - c > 0$. But this positive externality is not internalized by the retailer, who therefore has too low an incentive to expand the demand from the vertical structure's viewpoint. Further vertical control is then necessary to restore the appropriate incentive. At least three applications have been made of this idea,

---

[1] See the survey by Rey and Tirole (1986*a*) for a more complete treatment.

depending on the nature of the action chosen by the retailer. Suppose first that the action is the choice of the consumer price. Then the retailer chooses a price which is too high from the manufacturer's point of view (a high price reduces the demand for the good). This is the celebrated 'double marginalization' or 'chain-of-monopolies' problem (Spengler 1950). A price ceiling (RPM) eliminates the issue. Secondly, let the retailer choose a level of promotional services. In this case, the retailer tends to supply too low a level of services, thus contracting demand for the good. Thirdly, let the retailer's action be a technological choice. More precisely, suppose that the retailer (or, more generally, a downstream firm) uses two inputs, one of them being the manufacturer's good. Because of the mark-up $(p_w - c)$, the downstream unit substitutes towards the other input beyond what would be desirable from the vertical structure's point of view. Thus, productive inefficiency can be dissipated by using a tie-in. The manufacturer can require the downstream unit to buy *both* inputs from him. This allows him to inflate the price for the other input and restore the correct input-price ratio and production efficiency (see e.g. Blair and Kaserman 1978).

While these bilateral monopoly examples show that some restraints such as RPM or tie-ins can eliminate the basic vertical externality, they do not explain the emergence of such restraints. Indeed, there is a simpler way to deal with the problem. The manufacturer can charge a wholesale price equal to unit cost ($p_w - c = 0$), and make a profit through a franchise fee. He thus eliminates the externality, because the retailer becomes the residual claimant for any increase in demand (receives any increase in the vertical structure's profit). Note that such a two-part tariff is equivalent to selling the manufacturing technology to the retailer.[2]

Restricting the analysis to bilateral monopoly problems would, we believe, give an excessively rosy picture of vertical control. The demand contraction that hurts the manufacturer is also likely to hurt third parties. This is particularly clear when the variable chosen by the retailer is the consumer price or promotional effort. Correcting the vertical problem lowers the consumer's price and

[2] There are reasons, mainly linked with uncertainty, why franchise fees cannot in practice so easily solve the vertical control problem (see Tirole 1988: ch. 4). But such reasons should be incorporated into the analysis (rather than assuming franchise fees away).

raises promotional effort. Thus, both profit and consumer surplus increase. The picture is a bit more complex in our third example (input substitution). Let us simply note that the correction (be it a tie-in or a franchise fee) promotes an efficient mix of inputs, and thus reduces production costs. We will see that, by contrast, restraints that reduce competition between retailers may lower welfare.

As mentioned earlier, this survey discusses only restraints that are meant to reduce competition between the agents.[3] We distinguish between two types of competition: simultaneous and sequential. Section 2 looks at the private and social desirability of product market competition between retailers. Section 3 considers situations in which there is only one agent at a given instant, but this agent can be replaced over time (sequential competition). Section 4 offers some concluding remarks.

2. Simultaneous Competition

This section first describes a simple model, which demonstrates a trade-off involved in introducing competition between agents. It then analyses various aspects of this trade-off.

(a) Product Market Competition as an Incentive Device[4]

Consider a manufacturer choosing how to distribute his product in a given geographical area. Suppose he faces two possibilities: let several retailers compete; or give each a monopoly power on part of the market, i.e. an exclusive territory (alternatively, he could single out a single retailer to serve the whole area, the main point being that the retailer faces no competition). Suppose further that the manufacturer imposes a two-part tariff:[5] The transfer paid by each retailer is $A + p_w q$, where q is the quantity purchased, p_w the wholesale price, and A a franchise fee.

---

[3] In the conclusion, we mention a complementary literature on the link between restraints and competition between the 'principals'.

[4] The analysis here is drawn from Rey and Tirole 1986*b*.

[5] Ibid. informational assumptions are given that make a two-part tariff with or without exclusive territories the only feasible contracts.

To assess the (private) value of competition, the manufacturer must trade off two effects:

The 'efficiency effect'. This effect stems from the fact that competition destroys industry profits. For instance, two firms competing in a product market make less profit than they would make were they to form a single firm (co-ordinate their decisions). At worst, the merged firms could duplicate what they do in a competitive situation. In general, they can do even better. The efficiency effect calls for monopolization of the distribution sector through exclusive territories (if there are several distributors) or for a single distributor.

In the retailing context, it is easy to find examples of destructive competition (others will be given in the next subsection). Suppose that the retailers compete *à la* Bertrand (in prices). Assuming that the retailers are undifferentiated, the consumer price is equal to the wholesale price plus the marginal cost of distribution. There is no reason why this price coincides with that which would be chosen by a vertically integrated structure (that is, the wholesale price by itself is not sufficient to ensure the efficient exploitation of monopoly power through the retailers). In particular, with an uncertain environment, the consumer price, which is entirely cost-determined, does not react to changes in demand. It does react to the marginal cost of distribution, but not necessarily optimally (for instance, for linear demand, it reacts twice as much as would be optimal for the vertical structure).

The way to avoid the efficiency effect is to create a monopoly in distribution. Recall from our earlier discussion that making a monopoly retailer a residual claimant (by charging $p_w = c$) eliminates all distortions: a monopoly retailer facing the vertical structure's real marginal cost exploits the vertical structure's monopoly power optimally. The manufacturer can then use the franchise fee to recoup the expected profit.

The 'incentive effect'. While monopolization and residual claimancy exploit monopoly power efficiently, they also have the drawback of imposing too much risk on the retailer. The latter bears all the risk on demand and distribution costs, while the manufacturer does not bear any. Our previous remark that the manufacturer can appropriate the retailer's expected profit through a franchise fee is valid only if the retailer is risk-neutral. A risk-averse retailer values the right to buy the good at the production cost at less than the expected profit. How can the manufacturer share some of the risk with the retailer? Well, he can increase the wholesale price above the production cost and reduce the franchise fee accordingly. The retailer's profit then varies less with demand and distribution cost uncertainty. However, this insurance device reintroduces the basic vertical externality mentioned in the introduction. There is thus a conflict between insuring the retailer and giving him the right incentive to choose the consumer price.

Here enters competition. It is often claimed that product market competition can act as an incentive device. One way of formalizing this is as follows: maintain the assumption that the retailers compete in prices and are perfect substitutes (this is the archetypical model of competition). Suppose that the retailers face identical distribution cost shocks (they also face identical demand shocks because they serve the same market). Then, in Bertrand equilibrium, the consumer price is equal to the wholesale price plus the distribution cost, and both retailers make zero profit; retailers do not bear any risk in equilibrium![6] Competition yields insurance which, in turn, alleviates the incentive problem.

Remark: This model can easily be turned into one in which the consumer price is observable by the manufacturer, but the promotional effort is not. In an extreme case, promotional effort is a perfect substitute for price reduction. The incentive to choose the right price is then replaced by the incentive to exert the right promotional effort.

The resolution of the trade-off is easy to figure out. When the retailers do not fear risk, the manufacturer wants to foreclose the access of markets by assigning exclusive territories or by refusing to deal with more than one retailer. When the retailers are fairly risk averse, incentive problems become serious under monopolized retailing, and the manufacturer wants to introduce product market competition.

The optimal private arrangement, however, need not be socially optimal. The consumer surplus should also be taken into account. As can be shown under some reasonable assumptions, there is a tendency towards an excessive market foreclosure in this model in that the consumer surplus and aggregate welfare are higher under retailer competition. Exclusive territories or monopoly retailing yield a higher expected consumer price (because the manufacturer

---

[6] Note also that the franchise fee must be equal to zero under competition.

is forced to raise the wholesale price to insure retailers), as well as a socially sub-optimal sensitivity of consumer price to demand and cost uncertainty.[7]

(b) Further Drawbacks and Advantages of Product Market Competition

Here we briefly discuss the trade-off between downstream competition and monopoly in more general situations.

An explanation often advanced for competition-reducing restraints and, in particular, RPM, is the so-called free-rider problem (Telser 1960, Mathewson and Winter 1984, Perry and Porter 1986). The typical example is the case of a retailer providing pre-sale services (advising the consumers on the technology of stereo equipment or cameras) and losing the consumers, who then turn to a discount retailer. That is, retailers may free-ride on each other to supply the necessary information to consumers. In a competitive equilibrium, a low level of services is thus provided, harming both the manufacturer (the efficiency effect) and the consumers. Competition-reducing restraints (RPM, exclusive territories) may restore the incentive to supply retail services. For instance, the consumer has no incentive to obtain the information from one store and purchase from an equally priced competitor. This argument has recently been generalized to include quality certification by a reputable retailer.[8] The idea is that a retailer who is known to carry high-quality products conveys positive information to the consumers by introducing a new product into his product line. He will be willing, however, to perform this product-signalling function only if he derives a decent profit from it. This may call for suppression of competition: as in the previous free-riding argument, discounters may benefit from the product information conveyed by more expensive stores and attract consumers.[9]

---

[7] Similar conclusions can be drawn for RPM, another competition-reducing restraint.

[8] See the studies of Levi-Strauss and Oster and Florsheim Shoes by Greening in Lafferty *et al.* 1984. A formalization of the argument appears in Marvel and McCafferty 1984.

[9] Levi-Strauss used both RPM and dealer selection to market its jeans. A Federal Trade Commission order forbade Levi-Strauss to practise RPM, but allowed this manufacturer to continue selecting dealers on the basis of quality. For criticisms of the free-rider argument see Overstreet 1983 and Steiner 1985.

The free-rider argument and its generalization focus on a discussion of retailing quality that cannot be bundled with the retailer's product. Another branch of the literature ignores free-riding by assuming that quality cannot be unbundled from the product. Caillaud and Rey (1986) consider a single representative consumer model in which promotional effort is not a perfect substitute for a price reduction. They show that competition between retailers tends to lead to a 'wrong' quality-price mix offered to consumers,[10] another instance of the efficiency effect. Bolton and Bonanno (1988) introduce consumer diversity and study how the provision of different levels of services by different retailers may contribute to discrimination among consumers. In their model, the manufacturer is faced with two possible distortions. One is the familiar double marginalization discussed in the introduction. The other and newer distortion is a potentially inadequate choice of the quality spectrum by competing retailers. They study which panoplies of vertical restraints can eliminate these distortions.

We conclude that the competitive provision of services, be they tied to the product or not, in general do not suit the manufacturer's goals. The efficiency effect is thus pervasive.

Until now, we have considered retail competition as an endogenous institution. We must realize that there are instances in which the manufacturer has little choice but to allow retail competition. For one thing, retailers may be differentiated through location or services (as above), and thus the manufacturer may be better off having several of them in a given 'market'. Secondly, competition may not be avoidable. An interesting extension of the vertical restraint literature concerns *licensing* of a process innovation. Consider, for instance, the inventor of a new process that reduces production cost in an industry. Assuming that the inventor cannot exploit the innovation himself (this is not crucial), the issue is whether he will license to one or to several producers. It is analogous to the problem of a manufacturer deciding whether his product will be carried by one or several retailers in a given market. The process innovation is the good, the royalty fee is equivalent to

---

[10] More precisely, pure retail competition leads retailers to maximize consumer surplus given the wholesale price. By contrast, the vertical structure would like to maximize profit.

the wholesale price, and the fixed licensing fee corresponds to the franchise fee. There is a new twist, however; while the manufacturer may be able to create a monopoly on the retail market, the licensor may license a single licensee, but not prevent product market competition (its rivals may keep producing with the old technology).[11] In such a case, licensing to several producers results in a more efficient production structure, which may offset a potential increase in competition (see Kamien and Tauman 1983 and Katz and Shapiro 1985).[12]

3. Sequential Competition and Supplier Substitution

Another important kind of competition between agents is associated with the possibility of second-sourcing. There, the principal employs only one agent at a given date, but he may switch agents over time. This practice is used more or less frequently in defence contracting, in private contracting, and in regulated industries. One may think of at least two reasons why the principal may want to leave the door open to a second source: to exploit superior outside opportunities in the future, and to discipline the incumbent firm by the threat of a break-out. We examine these two motives and emphasize the private and social issues behind second-sourcing. In both cases, we consider models in which it is inefficient to have more than one agent produce at a given point in time.

(a) Foreclosing the Second Source

Aghion and Bolton (1987) have recently offered a simple and very useful analysis of how current contracting may bias future procurement choices against the second source (entrant). We sketch their model. Initially, a seller (the 'incumbent') and a buyer contract for the delivery of one unit of intermediate good. The buyer has a

[11] This situation would correspond to the non-franchised retailers pursuing the distribution of an inferior product in the retail market.

[12] An interesting incentive argument for competition has also been offered by Farrell and Gallini (1987) and Shepard (1987) in the context of licensing. Their theory holds that a manufacturer may license its technology to a rival in order to guarantee quality. Their framework is a Williamsonian one in which a user of the product must sink specific investments before obtaining the good. Once the investments are sunk, the monopoly supplier has an incentive to cut on quality; licensing guarantees quality competition *ex post*, and therefore gives the user better incentives to invest in the relationship.

unit demand for the intermediate good and has valuation 1 (alternatively, he could buy a backstop substitute at price 1). The seller's cost of producing this unit is ½. After the contract is signed, a competing supplier (the 'entrant') (unidentified at the date of the contract) will come up with a cost c of producing the good. Assume that c is a priori uniformly distributed between 0 and 1 (there is no loss of generality in assuming that an entrant appears; a high c *de facto* corresponds to no entry); assume further that c is known only to the entrant.

Consider first the optimal allocation for the integrated structure imposed by the incumbent and the buyer. Because the incumbent's cost (½) is lower than the buyer's valuation (1), the buyer always consumes one unit of the intermediate good. The issue is only to minimize the vertical structure's expected production cost. The trade-off is between producing internally at cost ½ or procuring from the entrant at a price p. This is a simple monopoly-pricing problem. The vertical structure minimizes

$$p\,\text{Prob}\{c \le p\} + \tfrac{1}{2}\,\text{Prob}\{c > p\} = p^2 + \tfrac{1}{2}(1 - p),$$

because the price offer to the incumbent p is accepted if and only if it exceeds c, and the distribution of c is uniform. This yields $p = \tfrac{1}{4}$. In the same way monopoly pricing leads to a welfare loss, the vertical structure's price offer to the entrant yields an inefficient production structure: when the entrant's cost lies between ¼ and ½, the incumbent supplies the intermediate good.

The next question is whether the integrated structure can realize the same outcome through a contract. To see that this is the case, suppose that the incumbent offers the following contract to the buyer: the buyer can buy from the incumbent at price ¾, the penalty for breach (liquidated damages) is equal to ½. Suppose further that the entrant makes the buyer an offer to breach from the incumbent (for simplicity we put the bargaining power on the entrant's side in its negotiation with the buyer). The buyer will accept such an offer only if it does not exceed ¾ − ½ = ¼. Thus, a profit-maximizing entrant makes an offer if and only if its cost is lower than ¼. Hence, the allocation and the vertical structure's expected profit are the same as in the integrated case. But we still have to address the possibility that the buyer may not want to accept a contract that helps the incumbent monopolize the intermediate good market. For this, we must specify what happens if the buyer rejects the incumbent's contract. Let us assume that if $c < \frac{1}{2}$, the entrant enters and Bertrand competition between the suppliers drives the price to $\frac{1}{2}$ (the entrant supplies). If $c \geqslant \frac{1}{2}$, the entrant does not enter. The incumbent then charges the monopoly price, 1, to the buyer. Thus, the expected price paid by the buyer is equal to $\frac{1}{2}(\frac{1}{2} + 1) = \frac{3}{4}$. But note that $\frac{3}{4}$ was also the expected price paid by the buyer under the contract offered by the incumbent. So the exclusionary contract is accepted by the buyer.[13]

Aghion and Bolton then analyse the externalities between several buyers (to abstract from downstream competition, let us assume that the buyers are in different industries or geographical markets). If the entrant produces under constant returns to scale (in particular, he does not face a fixed cost of entry or production, i.e. independent of the scale of operation), the buyers are somehow unrelated, and the contract signed between the incumbent and one buyer exerts no externality on the other buyers. The contract is then the same as in the one-buyer case. When the entrant faces a fixed cost, however, a buyer who signs a contract that reduces the entrant's profitability of dealing with him (because of penalties for breach) reduces the size of the entrant's market and thus the probability of entry. Because the fixed cost can only be recovered through mass production, a buyer's exclusivity or long-term contract exerts negative externalities on the other buyers.

An obvious observation is that the incumbent may be able to extract a lot of surplus from the individual buyers, while it could not do so if the latter colluded. To see why, suppose that there are a lot of small buyers, and suppose that the entrant's fixed cost is sufficiently large that entry to supply a single buyer is never profitable. Then, if all the other buyers accept a contract tying them to the incumbent, an individual buyer has no threat to turn to the entrant. The incumbent can then obtain the natural monopoly price (equal to 1). In general, however, the incumbent may offer a

---

[13] Two remarks are in order here. First, even if the incumbent has all the bargaining power in his negotiation with the buyer (i.e., makes a take-it-or-leave-it offer), it cannot realize the whole integrated structure's profit, equal to $\frac{9}{16}$. Its profit is equal to only $\frac{5}{16}$. This is because the buyer can threaten to get $\frac{1}{4}$ by rejecting the contract. Second, the exact division of surplus and the final allocation of production depends on the relative bargaining powers, and the assumption about price competition in case of rejection. But the incentive for the incumbent and the buyer to exploit their monopoly power *vis-à-vis* the entrant remains.

contract that allows the entrant to enter with some probability (as in the one-buyer case) and can do even better than a natural monopoly by extracting some of the efficiency gains from letting the entrant produce (as long as the buyers do not organize to synchronize their decisions).

(b) Incentives and Second Sourcing

Another point of using the threat of breaking out in favour of a second source may be to discipline a monopoly incumbent. Demski *et al.* (1987) in the context of regulation and Scharfstein (1988) in the context of take-overs (in which the agent is the incumbent management team and the second source a rival management team) have recently formalized this disciplinary role.[14] Their idea runs roughly as follows. Consider, for instance, a regulated monopoly which has private information about its production technology. This cost parameter can be 'high' or 'low'. Its cost depends on the cost parameter and on managerial effort (as well as possibly some random term). In the absence of a second source, this incumbent monopoly is given an incentive scheme by the regulator. He receives more when it produces at a lower cost. This incentive scheme is meant to induce the regulated firm to be efficient when its cost parameter is low, rather than claiming that the parameter is high and slacking. The 'incentive constraint', however, is costly. It excessively rewards the firm when it is efficient. Now, the threat of second-sourcing may alleviate this constraint. Suppose that when the firm produces at a cost which is supposed to reflect a high-cost parameter, the probability of replacing it by the entrant is higher than when the cost is lower.

This policy, of course, corresponds to efficiency precepts: the second source is more valuable when the incumbent firm is less efficient. But it also serves an incentive purpose by making it more costly for a low-cost incumbent to masquerade as a high-cost one. This comes from the fact that it is relatively harsher for a low-cost incumbent to be replaced by an entrant than for a high-cost incumbent because of the low-cost type's rent associated with asymmetric information. One of the main conclusions in Demski *et al.* (1987) and Scharfstein (1988) is that, under some conditions,

[14] See also Anton and Yao 1987 for a somewhat different model. Caillaud (1985) studies the case in which the principal cannot contract with a second source (competitive fringe).

the probability of replacing a high-cost incumbent by an entrant should be higher than it would be, were the regulator perfectly informed about the incumbent's technology (i.e. were the regulator guided solely by efficiency precepts). This is a formalization of the incentive argument. The regulator increases the probability of abandoning a high-cost firm to give incentives to the low-cost firm not to claim it has a high cost.[15]

Investment by the incumbent raises new issues (Williamson 1976). In particular, non-transferable investment is lost in case of a break-out. A transferable investment is not. However, as Williamson notes, investment is, in general, hard to measure accurately because of various accounting problems,[16] and it is therefore difficult to compensate the incumbent for his past investment in transferable assets. This yields too low an incentive for the incumbent to accumulate such assets.

Laffont and Tirole (1988a) study a two-period model in which investment is not directly observable. In the first period, the incumbent produces. The regulator observes the incumbent's realized cost, but cannot disentangle its various components: monetary investment, (managerial) cost-reducing effort, intrinsic productivity/efficiency (and possibly random elements). In the second period, the regulator must decide whether to stick to the incumbent or to switch to a second source. Part of the incumbent's investment is transferable to the second source, the other part is not.

A natural bench-mark when studying the optimal break-out policy is the notion of bidding parity. Bidding parity holds if the entrant is chosen if and only if he is intrinsically more efficient in the second period than the incumbent (note that each firm's second-period efficiency depends on the incumbent's first-period investment). If bidding parity does not hold, the regulator may favour the incumbent or the entrant at the renewal stage. For instance, in the

---

[15] The two papers also consider the case in which the incumbent's and the entrant's technologies are positively correlated. There is a new informational effect. The entrant's technology then brings information on (and hence allows an improved monitoring of) the incumbent's technology. See also our concluding remarks on tournaments.

[16] On the one hand, the investment may be non-monetary. On the other hand, the incumbent can inflate the price of his investments and arrange kickbacks (possibly through other contracts) from his suppliers, or else he can vertically integrate.

investment-free models of Demski *et al.* (1987) and Scharfstein (1988) bidding parity does not hold, as the entrant is favoured.

The nature of the optimal deviation from bidding parity depends on the type of investment. For *transferable* investments, the incumbent should be favoured at the renewal stage. The intuition is that the incumbent tends to invest socially too little in transferable investments: by investing more, the incumbent exerts a positive externality on the entrant if the latter is chosen.[17] For *non-transferable* investments, it can be shown that the entrant should be favoured.

The destruction of bidding parity is not the only consequence of the existence of investment. For transferable investment, the incumbent is also induced to (partly) internalize the positive externality on the entrant through a time-increasing slope of his incentive scheme (optimal incentive schemes turn out to be linear in cost in this model). He is encouraged to invest if he bears a low fraction of investment cost and receives a high fraction of the future cost savings.

There is also an important distinction between monetary investment (which we just considered) and investments in human capital. Suppose, for instance, that the first-period managerial effort decreases not only the first-period cost, but also the second-period one (learning by doing). The first-period effort can be considered an investment but, contrary to investments in machines, say, it does not raise the first-period cost. It can be shown that learning by doing also creates a bias toward the incumbent. Favouring the incumbent in the second period gives him a further incentive to invest in learning by doing. This reduces the first-period cost, which is valuable to the regulator who shares part of this cost.[18]

Overall, these conclusions confirm Williamson's pessimism about the possibility of second-sourcing when substantial investments are at stake. Of the three effects playing against bidding

---

[17] One way of encouraging the incumbent to invest is to offer to reimburse the totality of its costs in the first period. The incumbent then does not mind investing. Furthermore, he has no incentive to invest too much if its second period cost is fully reimbursed (assuming its contract is renewed). However, such 'cost-plus' contracts are too costly because of moral hazard. The firm's managers have every incentive to slack if the costs are fully passed on to the regulator.

[18] It can further be shown that the optimal contracts are linear in the firms' cost overruns.

parity, only one tends to favour the entrant, and it operates only for non-transferable investments; but, for such investments, the incumbent's contract is likely to be renewed anyway because the entrant has a serious cost disadvantage at the second-period bidding stage.

This second-sourcing literature has been mainly cast in a regulatory set-up. But the same principles apply to relationships between private firms and their suppliers. The implication in this context is that the previous Aghion and Bolton conclusion of excessive market foreclosure through long-term contracting will be difficult to apply in real-world situations involving substantial investments. Long-term contracts (or, more generally, contracts that favour the incumbent in the future) may be desirable to give the incumbents an adequate incentive to invest. In practice, it may be hard to determine whether a long-term contract is meant to foreclose the market or to promote efficient investment.[19]

4. Concluding Remarks

In this brief survey, we discussed the private and social desirability of competition between agents. Two other topics dealing with competition in vertical structures would have been worth reviewing.

First, we have focused on direct competition: product market competition in section 2 and supplier substitution in section 3. In both cases, the agents are competing either for the same consumers or for the same buyer. There is also an indirect method of competition between agents, called yardstick competition.[20] The idea is that agents face similar environments, so that one agent's performance can be used to learn about another agent's environment and thus reduce informational asymmetries and improve incentives. Note that the agents need not be competing on the product market. For instance, one can envision two salespersons

---

[19] Our model has presumed complete contracts. There is also a large literature on incomplete contracts and long-term relationships. See e.g. Williamson 1975, 1985 and Grossman and Hart 1986 on how specific investments might be jeopardized by short-run contracting, and Laffont and Tirole 1988b on why the incumbent may not want to demonstrate efficiency because of the 'ratchet effect' (according to which a good performance today triggers a demanding incentive scheme in the future).

[20] See Baiman and Demski 1980, Holmström 1982, Lazear and Rosen 1981, Nalebuff and Stiglitz 1983, and Shleifer 1985.

operating in two distinct (exclusive) territories, with correlated demands in these two geographical areas.[21]

Last, there is an interesting and rapidly expanding literature on the case in which the agents are agents for different principals. Bonanno and Vickers (1988) and Rey and Stiglitz (1986) show how vertical restraints may soften upstream competition. Mathewson and Winter (1985) analyse exclusive dealing as a way to eliminate upstream competition. Fershtman and Judd (1986) and Katz (1987) offer general models of competition between principals via agents. On a different issue, we should also mention Bernheim and Whinston's work on common agency (1986) (which features a single agent contracting with several principals).

As we see, much progress has been made in the study of incentives and competition. But the theory is still in its infancy, and we expect and hope that the next years will bring more realistic and general formalizations of these issues, as well as further applications.

---

[21] Yardsticking may also be mixed with product market competition. For instance, the performance of GM managers can be compared by the GM shareholders to that of Ford managers.

References

Aghion, P. and Bolton, P. (1987), 'Contracts as a Barrier to Entry', *American Economic Review*, 77: 388–401.

Anton, J. J. and Yao, D. A. (1987), 'Second Sourcing and the Experience Curve: Price Competition in Defense Procurement', *Rand Journal of Economics*, 18: 57–76.

Baiman, S. and Demski, J. (1980), 'Economically Optimal Performance Evaluation and Control Systems', *Journal of Accounting Research* (Supplement).

Bernheim, D. and Whinston, M. (1986), 'Common Agency', *Econometrica*, 54: 923–42.

Blair, R. and Kaserman, D. (1978), 'Vertical Integration, Tying and Antitrust Policy', *American Economic Review*, 68: 397–402.

Bolton, P. and Bonanno, G. (1988), 'Vertical Restraints in a Model of Vertical Differentiation', *Quarterly Journal of Economics*, 103: 555–70.

Bonanno, G. and Vickers, J. (1988), 'Vertical Separation', *Journal of Industrial Economics*, 36: 257–65.

Caillaud, B. (1985), 'Regulation, Competition, and Asymmetric Information', *Journal of Economic Theory* (forthcoming).

—— and Rey, P. (1986), 'A Note on Vertical Restraints with the Provision of Distribution Services', mimeo. INSEE and MIT.

Demski, J., Sappington, D., and Spiller, P. (1987), 'Managing Supplier Switching', *Rand Journal of Economics*, 18: 77–97.

Farrell, J. and Gallini, N. (1987), 'Second-Sourcing as a Commitment: Monopoly Incentives to Attract Competition', *Rand Journal of Economics*.

Fershtman, C. and Judd, K. (1986), 'Strategic Incentive Manipulation in Rivalrous Agency', IMSSS TR 496, Stanford University.

Grossman, S. and Hart, O. (1986), 'The Costs and Benefits of Ownership: A Theory of Vertical and Lateral Integration', *Journal of Political Economy*, 94: 691–719.

Holmström, B. (1982), 'Moral Hazard in Teams', *Bell Journal of Economics*, 13: 324–40.

Kamien, M. and Tauman, Y. (1983), 'The Private Value of a Patent: A Game Theoretic Analysis', Northwestern University DP 576.

Katz, M. (1987), 'Game-Playing Agents: Contracts as Precommitments', mimeo., Princeton University.

—— and Shapiro, C. (1985), 'On the Licensing of Innovations', *Rand Journal of Economics*, 16: 504–20.

Lafferty, R., Lande, R., and Kirkwood, J. (eds.) (1984), *Impact Evaluation of Federal Trade Commission Vertical Restraints Cases*, US Federal Trade Commission.

Laffont, J.-J. and Tirole, J. (1988a), 'Repeated Auctions of Incentive Contracts, Investment, and Bidding Parity', *Rand Journal of Economics*, 19: 516–37.

—— and —— (1988b), 'The Dynamics of Incentive Contracts', *Econometrica*, 56: 1153–77.

Lazear, E. and Rosen, S. (1981), 'Rank-Order Tournaments as Optimum Labor Contracts', *Journal of Political Economy*, 89: 841–64.

Marvel, H. and McCafferty, S. (1984), 'Resale Price Maintenance and Quality Certification', *Rand Journal of Economics*, 55: 346–59.

Mathewson, F. and Winter, R. (1984), 'An Economic Theory of Vertical Restraints', *Rand Journal of Economics*, 55: 27–38.

—— and —— (1985), 'Is Exclusive Dealing Anti-Competitive?' Working Paper 8517, University of Toronto.

Nalebuff, B. and Stiglitz, J. (1983), 'Information Competition and Markets', *American Economic Review, Papers and Proceedings*, 73: 278–84.

Overstreet, T. (1983), *Resale Price Maintenance: Economic Theories and Empirical Evidence*, US Federal Trade Commission.

Perry, M. and Porter, R. (1986), 'Resale Price Maintenance and Exclusive Territories in the Presence of Retail Service Externalities', mimeo., Bell Core.

Rey, P. and Stiglitz, J. (1986), 'The Role of Exclusive Territories in Producers' Competition', mimeo., Princeton University.

—— and Tirole, J. (1986a), 'Vertical Restraints from a Principal-Agent Viewpoint', in L. Pellegrini and S. Reddy (eds.), *Marketing Channels: Relationships and Performance*, Lexington Books, Lexington, Mass.

—— and —— (1986b), 'The Logic of Vertical Restraints', *American Economic Review*, 76: 921–39.

Scharfstein, D. (1988), 'The Disciplinary Role of Takeovers', *Review of Economic Studies*, 55: 185–200.

Shepard, A. (1987), 'Licensing to Enhance Demand for New Technologies', *Rand Journal of Economics*, 18: 360–8.

Shleifer, A. (1985), 'A Theory of Yardstick Competition', *Rand Journal of Economics*, 16: 319–27.

Spengler, J. (1950), 'Vertical Integration and Antitrust Policy', *Journal of Political Economy*, 58: 347–52.

Steiner, R. (1985), 'The Nature of Vertical Restraints', *Antitrust Bulletin*, 30: 143–97.

Telser, L. (1960), 'Why Should Manufacturers Want Fair Trade?' *Journal of Law and Economics*, 3: 86–105.

Tirole, J. (1988), *The Theory of Industrial Organization*, MIT Press, Cambridge, Mass.

Williamson, O. (1975), *Markets and Hierarchies: Analysis and Antitrust Implications*, Free Press, New York.

—— (1976), 'Franchise Bidding for Natural Monopoly', *Bell Journal of Economics*, 7: 73–104.

—— (1985), *The Economic Institutions of Capitalism*, Free Press, New York.

6

New Theories of Predatory Pricing[1]

Paul Milgrom and John Roberts

With the approach of 1992, when EEC regulations will prevail in any Common Market member not having its own national competition policy, antitrust issues have become a subject of immediate interest in a number of European countries. At the same time, concerns with 'international competitiveness' have reinvigorated the debate over antitrust in North America and elsewhere in the industrialized world. This renewed interest in competition policy coincides with an unparalleled series of advances in economists' theoretical understanding of the competitive, strategic behaviour of firms and of the welfare implications of this behaviour. This new learning can potentially inform the formulation of policy in important ways. The purpose of this chapter is to review one aspect of this work and point out its implications for antitrust policy.

The subject at hand is predatory pricing, the temporary charging of particularly low prices in order to improve long-run profitability by inducing exit, deterring entry, or 'disciplining' rivals into accepting relatively small market shares. The idea that firms might use such pricing practices as an exclusionary device is a familiar one. Well-documented instances of this practice date back over a century, and claims of recent occurrences continue. For over three-quarters of a century, both explicit legislation and case law in the USA have condemned such temporary price cutting, at least when practised by large firms or ones that already hold significant market shares. Yet, despite the widespread belief in the existence and efficacy of predatory pricing, the logic of this alleged practice was not subjected to adequately reasoned legal or economic analysis until McGee's influential 1958 re-examination of the *Standard Oil* case.[2]

[1] The financial support of the National Science Foundation is gratefully acknowledged.
[2] *Standard Oil Company of New Jersey* v. *U.S.*, 221 U.S. 1, 47, 76 (1911).

This case was brought under Section 2 of the Sherman Antitrust Act of 1890, which forbids attempts to monopolize.[3] The claim was that the Standard Oil Trust had attempted in the period up to 1899 to obtain a monopoly position and that it had done so in part through a policy of selective price cutting aimed at rivals in particular markets. Standard Oil was supposed to have cut prices and held them low until the targeted rivals were forced to exit or agreed to sell out to Rockefeller. (Other alleged exclusionary tactics included the securing of preferential rail rates, foreclosing supplies to rivals, industrial espionage, and the selective use of dynamite on rivals' facilities.) Other well-documented instances of such apparent predation from the same era involve ocean shipping in the China–United Kingdom tea trade (see Yamey 1972, for a description based on the House of Lords investigation in the *Mogul* case) and the United States Tobacco Trust (see Burns 1986 and 1987). Based on such cases, the idea of predatory pricing became well established in legal, business, and economic thinking, and it remains so today. For example, see the recent claims of predatory pricing in the 'less-than-truckload' motor-carrier industry in the Eastern Central states in the period since trucking deregulation (Abruzzese 1987) or the recent complaints about 'dumping' (e.g. of semiconductors by Hitachi in the United States or of automobiles by Hyundai in Canada).

In this context, it is striking that McGee argued that predatory pricing was not a rational strategy for Rockefeller's firm to have adopted. Further, although various authors suggested potential difficulties with McGee's original arguments or their extension to other cases (e.g. Telser 1966; Scherer 1970; Yamey 1972; Posner 1976), even quite recently McGee was able to argue forcefully that predatory pricing was very unlikely to yield a positive return, that it would thus rarely be adopted, that the main effect of legal prohibitions would be to deter desirable price competition, and, moreover, that no satisfactory, complete economic analysis indicated otherwise (McGee 1980).

[3] This is still the usual vehicle for bringing predatory pricing cases in the US. Exceptions come in regulated industries in which specific statutes give antitrust exemption but still outlaw predatory pricing. For example, the use of 'fighting ships' is expressly condemned by the Shipping Act 1916, which otherwise gives a measure of antitrust immunity to the regulated ocean liner shipping industry. Section 86 of the Treaty of Rome appears to provide a basis for prosecuting predatory pricing in the EEC.

McGee's key arguments may be summarized as follows.[4] First, he argued that driving out rivals via predation does not prevent new entry from occurring once the predator raises its prices to enjoy its improved market position, and such entry (whether by new firms or the erstwhile prey) may in fact be made easy because the prey's production facilities will be available. Such entry means that any gains from inducing exit will be short-lived. Secondly, McGee suggested that cheaper strategies for achieving a monopoly are often available. For example, merger or acquisition would have been legal options in Rockefeller's time, and the relatively relaxed attitude of the Reagan administration on antitrust has again made concentration-increasing mergers easier. Thirdly, McGee claimed that predatory pricing ought not to be able to force exit, once the fact that the price cutting must be temporary is recognized. The prospect of long-term profitability ought to lead the prey to stay in, and ought to give its investors and lenders the incentive to finance any temporary losses.

McGee's arguments would suggest a legal doctrine that presumes that claims of predation are without merit. While economic reasoning has had an increasing impact on the thinking of lawyers and judges in the United States, few have fully accepted the implications of McGee's work. Instead, the emerging orthodoxy in United States antitrust law is based on a literature that appeared between McGee's two papers and that largely ignored his arguments. This literature continues to assume that predatory pricing is a potential problem because it might be used as an exclusionary device. It then seeks to determine legal tests that would establish that predation had been attempted. The key feature of this work is an objective of avoiding having to determine judicially the intent of the accused firm's pricing policy and, instead, of substituting mechanical examination of quantities that are presumed to be objectively observable, such as prices, costs, or output levels.

The leading contribution to this literature—both in terms of its temporal precedence and its impact on US case law—is that of Areeda and Turner (1975).[5] The Areeda–Turner test is conceptually simple: prices above (reasonably anticipated) marginal cost represent legal competitive behaviour; prices below marginal cost

---

[4] A fuller discussion and references to development of McGee's ideas by others may be found in Milgrom (1987).

[5] See Ordover and Saloner (1987) for a presentation and extended critique of both the Areeda–Turner test and its principal competitors.

represent illegal predation. The apparent simplicity of this test and its connection to the theory of perfectly competitive behaviour (and, by extension, to Pareto optimality criteria) have been central to its becoming the key element of the new orthodoxy.

Since 1982, however, a new literature in economics has emerged that re-examines the logic of predatory pricing and of predatory or exclusionary practices more generally. This work involves strategic, game-theoretic analyses of imperfectly competitive behaviour, in contrast to the more standard (non-strategic) economic logic that is embodied in both McGee and Areeda–Turner. Significantly, this new research undermines the conclusions of both the competing branches of previous work: predatory pricing can make excellent theoretical sense, and yet the predatory prices bear no necessary relation to marginal costs.

In the remainder of this paper we briefly describe some of the major elements of this new work. We focus on models where predation arises in response to informational asymmetries and especially on ones where it manifests itself as an attempt to affect rivals' perceptions and inferences about future profits.[6] Our discussion will attempt to relate this literature to more familiar themes by accentuating the market structure assumptions in the theoretical models. A second focus is on the predictions that emerge from these models concerning the relationships between prices and costs under predatory behaviour. Finally, we offer some thoughts regarding the policy implications of this work.

1. Intertemporal Demand Linkages and Predation

Although our focus is on models of predation in which informational asymmetries are fundamental, in this section we digress briefly to discuss theories in which intertemporal linkages in demand underlie predation.

Recall McGee's argument that any gains from predation will be fleeting at best and thus that it will rarely be worth while to suffer reductions in current profits to induce exit: the predator's raising prices above costs to enjoy the increased market power that it

[6] Fuller discussions of this strand of the literature are found in Ordover and Saloner (1987) and Roberts (1987), and a critique of the methodology of games of incomplete information as it is used in these models is found in Milgrom and Roberts (1987).

bought by preying will attract new entry (or re-entry). For this argument to be valid, it must be the case that entrants will be able to compete on a more-or-less equal footing with the incumbent. Under the assumptions embodied in standard models, this is indeed the case: sales in one period have no impact on future demands or costs, so new entrants are not disadvantaged relative to established firms. If, however, these conditions fail, then McGee's argument fails too, and predation that did induce exit might well give rise to permanently increased market share and supernormal returns. For example, if there are strong experience curve effects, then late entrants will suffer a production cost disadvantage that may prevent their competing effectively, or if customers incur significant costs in changing brands, then late entrants are handicapped by their need either to compensate customers for these switching costs or to limit themselves to buyers who had not been served by the incumbent.

A number of authors have examined the dynamics of competition in the presence of such inter-temporal linkages. See, for example, Fudenberg and Tirole (1983) on learning curves and Klemperer (1986) on switching costs. However, relatively little attention has been given to the possibility of predatory practices in these contexts. An important exception is due to Farrell and Saloner (1986), who focus on situations where technological compatibility concerns create externalities in demand that provide a basis for rational predation. (See also Katz and Shapiro 1986.)

Consider a durable good whose value to any individual user is an increasing function of the number of individuals using it: a computer employing a particular operating system is a possible example. Suppose (individually infinitesimal) customers arrive at a rate $n(t)$, and that once they purchase, they are 'locked in'. Suppose too that at some date T^*, a new product appears that fills the same function as the existing product but is technologically incompatible with it. Newly arriving customers after date T^* can select either product, and the benefits that accrue at any date to a customer from having made either choice are an increasing function of the total mass of customers having made the same choice by that date.

In such a situation, it will be an equilibrium for all customers arriving after date T^* to select the new technology if the discounted present value of being the first to adopt it, assuming that all later arrivals follow suit, exceeds the discounted present value of being the last to adopt the old technology. If this inequality is reversed, then the unique equilibrium is for no one to adopt the new technology. (See Farrell and Saloner 1986 for a full characterization of equilibrium.)

Now, suppose that the new technology is competitively supplied, so that it is priced so that its vendors earn zero profits, while a monopoly exists in the existing technology, and further suppose that, under monopoly pricing of the existing technology, it is equilibrium behaviour for the new technology to supplant the old. However, suppose that the new technology is not that much superior to the old, and, in particular, that there is a non-negative price for the product embodying old technology at which, at date T^*, it is better to be the last buying this product than the first buying into the new technology, even if all later puchasers should also adopt the new technology. In this case, it is feasible for the monopolist to cut its price to this level and deter the buyers at T^* from adopting the new technology. Moreover, suppose the mono- polist continues to hold its price down. Then eventually (but in finite time) a sufficient mass of customers will have purchased its product that the benefits for new buyers of having compatibility with this large installed base are sufficient that the unique equilibrium from that date on is for all new arrivals to choose the old technology, even if it is monopolistically priced. From this point on, the monopolist can keep its price at the monopoly level[7] without fear of anyone choosing the new technology. Thus, predation is feasible, and it may also be profitable if price does not have to be cut too much for too long, i.e. if the new technology is not too much better than the old.

Note that there is no reason to expect that the predatory pricing in this model would necessarily involve prices below marginal or average variable costs (either those of the monopolist or those of the competitive purveyors of the new product). Thus, such predation would not run afoul of the Areeda–Turner test. Moreover, as Farrell and Saloner suggest, it is even possible that this form of predation may be welfare-enhancing in that, absent

---

[7] During the predatory period, the price needed to deter adoption gradually rises to the monopoly level as the installed base grows.

predation, equilibrium might involve adoption of the new technology when the socially efficient outcome would be for the older technology to prevail.[8]

These features—that predation may be rational, that cost-based tests may fail to identify this predatory behaviour, and that the predation may be socially desirable—reappear in the information-based analyses discussed below. Meanwhile, given the frequency of complaints about predatory dumping in industries with strong experience-curve effects (e.g. DRAM semiconductor chips), and the common use of cost-based criteria to judge whether illegal pricing is being practised, it would seem valuable to see if these conclusions hold in a context where sales volume has intertemporal cost implications.

2.   Predation as Driving a Rival into Bankruptcy

The standard image of predatory pricing is probably best captured by the 'long-purse' or 'deep-pockets' story: a firm with greater financial resources cuts price enough to impose losses on its weaker rivals, who eventually are forced to exit by impending or actual bankruptcy that occurs while the predator is still comfortably solvent. The predator then raises price again to enjoy its monopoly. Presumably, monopoly profits from other product or geographic markets would be a source of the war chest needed to pursue this strategy. Thus, this view of predation naturally becomes associated with the image of a large firm operating in several (product or geographic) markets preying upon a smaller one operating in few markets, even if the prey has the larger market share in the contested markets (as in the *Utah Pie*[9] case).

In fact, the basic idea behind the long-purse/deep-pocket story— that predation involves imposing losses and ultimate bankruptcy— has until very recently lacked acceptable theoretical underpinnings, despite some important attempts to build a theory involving these elements.

---

[8] The key externality here is that those who have already adopted the old technology are marooned when the new one supplants it, and they receive fewer benefits than they would if later purchasers' choices were to be compatible with them.

[9] *Utah Pie Co.* v. *Continental Baking Co. et al.* 386 U.S. 685, 697 (1967).

Telser (1966) was the first to show formally that differential ability to sustain losses can, indeed, make it rational to bankrupt a rival if this will yield a sufficient stream of monopoly profits (and if merger is not a cheaper alternative). However, his analysis simply assumed that one firm has a larger war chest. In particular, it does not explain why the prey cannot borrow funds to obtain a similar-sized war chest. Note that the mere availability of such funds would deter a firm's rival from ever attempting to bankrupt it through predation, and so the potential prey would never actually have to call upon its line of credit. Moreover, if such borrowing is not possible, then within the terms of Telser's model the prey should recognize its weakness and the predator's incentives and should exit before (or at least as soon as) predation is adopted, since this minimizes its losses. (This point is made very clearly by Benoit (1984).) Thus, this model predicts that actual predation ought never to be observed, except as a result of mistakes.

Later contributions sought to overcome these problems in the theory, but with only limited success. In particular, Benoit (1984) showed that assuming asymmetric information regarding the prey's commitment to the business can alter the model's predictions so as both to rationalize continued operation in the face of predation and to generate actual predatory episodes. Specifically, suppose that the potential prey alone knows how long a period of losses it can survive. Suppose too that there is some chance that the prey will stubbornly stay in until destroyed, but that the predator cannot tell if its prey is committed to this line of behaviour. Finally, assume (as in Telser's model) that re-entry after exit is not possible. Consider now a firm that is a normal profit-maximizer. When faced by predation, it could initially mimic the behaviour of the committed and stay in, despite incurring losses, in the hope that the predator will become pessimistic about the possibility of inducing exit at reasonable cost and will acquiesce to the prey's continued existence. If this continued existence is sufficiently profitable, then the prey will be willing to purchase it by suffering the losses involved in staying in the market in the face of predation. Thus, the mere threat of predation (or a single episode of unremuneratively low pricing) does not necessarily induce exit. Meanwhile, it can still be in the predator's interest to cut prices because exit can be induced, although perhaps not immediately. Thus, one would observe predatory incidents, these would be of varying lengths, and they could end either by the prey's exiting or by the predator's giving up the fight.

While these predictions seem attractive and this general line of argument has some real appeal, the specific form of informational asymmetry assumed by Benoit is not particularly natural. Firms might well be unsure about how great their rivals' reserves are, about the losses that others will incur at different prices, or about how much each is willing to suffer to achieve a monopoly position. If informational asymmetries of these sorts alone could be shown to generate predatory episodes in equilibrium, the theory would have much more appeal than it does when it has to rely on the possibility of suicidal stubbornness or stupidity. Unfortunately, it is not obvious that these more plausible asymmetries will suffice. Moreover, Benoit's model still leaves unanswered the objection to assuming, rather than explaining, differential ability to absorb losses.

Fudenberg and Tirole (1985) have suggested a different approach that seeks the dual objective of both meeting the objection that the prey ought to be able to borrow funds to finance its defence and, at the same time, of generating an equilibrium in which actual predatory behaviour would occur. Suppose that there is a moral hazard problem with borrowers' possibly misappropriating funds. Then, results in the theory of contracts (Townsend 1979; Gale and Hellwig 1985) indicate that the amount that a firm will be able to borrow in any period under the optimal one-period contract will depend positively on the amount of its own capital that it can put up in the period. Thus, eroding a firm's reserves sufficiently by imposing losses on it may result in its losing further access to the capital market. At this point it could presumably be driven into bankruptcy by further below-cost pricing. Then, recognizing its vulnerability, it would leave.

This suggestion is interesting, but far from completely worked out. In particular, it does not allow for the possibility of the target firm's obtaining multiperiod financing arrangements under which it would retain access to additional capital even if its assets were depleted by predatory pricing. If such were available, then predation would again be ineffective, because eroding the prey's capital would not deny it access to further funding and so not put it in a position where it could be bankrupted. It is certainly plausible that contracts that would guarantee enough access to borrowing to deter predation would be unfeasible because they would be subject to such great incentives for misappropriation. However, absent a demonstration of this, the long-purse/deep-pocket story could not be considered to hold together theoretically.

Very recently, Bolton and Scharfstein (1988) have largely met these objections. They consider a situation very much like that treated by Fudenberg and Tirole. Two firms compete for two periods. One has access to internally generated funds to finance its operation while the other has no such access (in either period) and so must rely on borrowed capital. Again, a large firm operating in several markets and a small, local firm seem to provide a natural context for application. The profits of the second firm can take on one of two values ('High' or 'Low'), and their realized value is not directly observable to lenders. Thus, these profits may potentially be misappropriated by the owner/managers, who can simply claim that profits are low when they are actually high.[10] Finally, the first firm can take actions that increase the probability that the second firm's profits will be low. These are not specifically modelled (pricing is suppressed in this model), but presumably cutting price is a major candidate for this role.

Bolton and Scharfstein first consider the optimal financing contract between the capital market and the second firm under the assumption that predation will not be practised. They show that the optimal contract makes the probability of obtaining financing for the second period an increasing function of first-period announced profits, since this gives the firm an incentive not to misappropriate first-period receipts.[11] Of course, this gives an incentive for predation (provided the cost of preying is low enough), since increasing the probability of the low-profit outcome increases the likelihood that the second firm will not be active in the second period because it will be unable to gain financing.[12]

[10] The authors also suggest that their model would apply in other moral-hazard contexts, for instance, where effort that (probabilistically) increases profits is unobservable by investors and costly for managers to provide.

[11] In equilibrium, misappropriation is fully deterred, so that—assuming equilibrium behaviour—the lenders can infer that low profits are a result only of bad luck and not of managerial moral hazard. Still, the costly punishment of (probabilistically) denying credit must be inflicted in order to maintain incentives.

[12] Note that there is no way in this model to prevent misappropriation in the last period, because the firm has no assets that can be seized. Thus, if one lender cuts off credit, no other will lend (provided the low level of profits is negative). In contrast, Fudenberg and Tirole assume in their single-period model that the lowest level of profit is positive, so that there is something to seize.

Bolton and Scharfstein then calculate the optimal contract between the second firm and its lenders subject to a constraint that predation not be attractive. The effect of this constraint is straightforward: to deter predation, it is necessary to reduce the difference between the probabilities of refinancing for the second period when profits are high versus when they are low.[13] This can occur by lowering the probability of refinancing when profits are high, but may also take the form of increasing the probability of refinancing after low profits are reported.

Whether deterring predation is actually worth while depends on the value of various parameters in the model and on whether the financing contract is observed by the potential predator. Nevertheless, there are situations in which equilibrium involves predation, even when the prey has access to multiperiod financing arrangements. Of course, for costly predation to be adopted in equilibrium, it must bring a positive pay-off in terms of increased exit.

Note that the results of this modelling do not quite correspond to the usual deep-pocket story, because the predation does not have the effect of exhausting the prey's resources and thus forcing exit (as in Fudenberg and Tirole 1985); instead, the low profits it yields lead to credit being cut off. This is not *per se* a criticism of the model, since the traditional story ignores the possibility of borrowing, but it would be interesting to examine whether the original story can be made rigorous. It is also worth noting that the Bolton-Scharfstein results depend on the lenders not being able to determine that predation has been practised[14] and so on their not being more willing to refinance if low profits arise during a predatory episode than if predation has not been practised. Nevertheless, it seems likely that the broad outlines of their results would continue to be valid so long as the lenders cannot be certain that predation has occurred.

However, note that if the lenders can monitor managerial behaviour sufficiently well, they can reduce or eliminate the asymmetries of information that underlie this whole approach. These features may help explain the frequent practice of the providers of financing having a membership on corporate boards.

---

[13] Again, it is a property of the optimal contract that profits are correctly reported.

[14] Even though they may be able to infer that it has occurred under the assumption of equilibrium behaviour.

Moreover, venture capitalists, who provide funding to start-up firms, often take a quite active role in working with management. To the extent that monitoring may be easiest in such presumably small firms, the assumptions of this model may be less applicable here than would otherwise be the case.

The importance of these results is that the long-purse/deep-pocket story of predation is the only one in which imposing losses on a current rival—and thus below-cost pricing—plays any central, necessary role. As we shall see, modern, inference-based theories of predation involve much more subtle modes of behaviour, with the predation taking the form of using low prices to attempt to alter rivals' beliefs and expectations and thereby induce exit, deter entry, or limit their aggressiveness. The predatory behaviour in these models need not involve prices that are less than costs. However, even in the deep-pocket approach, there would seem to be no implication that price will be below *marginal* cost; all that is needed is that there be a negative cash flow. Moreover, it is the costs of the alleged prey, not those of the predator, that are relevant. The implications for the Areeda-Turner orthodoxy are clear, although we will belabour them below.

3. Predation as Pricing to Influence Expectations

A firm's decisions about entering or leaving an industry, about accepting or rejecting a merger offer, or about setting its prices or determining its output are all properly based on its expectations of the profit implications of these various choices. If a rival could influence these expectations, then it could affect the firm's decisions. For example, if an incumbent firm could cause potential entrants to believe that it would be an especially tough firm against which to compete, it might deter their entry. And if charging particularly low prices could lead to such beliefs, we would then have a theory of limit or predatory pricing. Similarly, if preying upon one entrant would deter other potential entrants because they expect to meet the same reception, then we would have another theoretical basis for predatory behaviour.

However, under the informational and behavioural assumptions that are commonly (if sometimes only implicitly) made in standard economic modelling—that all relevant information is equally well (or poorly) observed by everyone, that agents ignore sunk costs and benefits and, in each situation, act in the fashion that is optimal from that point forward, and that optimal behaviour is uniquely identified in each situation—it turns out to be remarkably difficult to construct an equilibrium theory in which agents are able to manipulate one another's beliefs. The reason is that with symmetric information every agent can figure out what is optimal for each to do, because each knows the others' objectives, capabilities, and options as well as they do. Thus, each can predict exactly what equilibrium behaviour will be from each point forward, and with unique equilibria there is no room for non-trivial expectations that involve anything manipulable by an agent.

However, once agents are differentially informed, matters change markedly.[15] The literature in fact contains a variety of models in which asymmetric information gives rise to the use of aggressively low prices and high outputs to attempt to influence rivals' behaviour through their beliefs. Traditionally, these models have been viewed as falling into three classes—labelled 'signalling', 'signal-jamming', and 'reputation' models, respectively—and the three do in fact have some different characteristics and different implications. Nevertheless, all three are fundamentally manifestations of the same basic phenomenon, and although we will respect the traditional labels, this underlying unity should be kept in mind (see Milgrom and Roberts 1987).

We consider signalling models first. These models rely on the predator being better informed than the prey about some market characteristics that are relevant to the prey's exit and output decisions. For example, suppose a firm's costs are private information to it. Because the firm's costs are uncertain from the point of view of its current or potential rivals, even if they could accurately predict how the firm's price and output will depend on its cost (the firm's strategy)—as they can in equilibrium—they cannot predict what its actual choices will be and thus what profits they will earn

[15] One could also possibly build a theory of predatory or limit pricing without assuming asymmetric information by relaxing the uniqueness of equilibrium assumption. Specifically, low prices could possibly be a means to indicate that the prey should expect that, if it does not exit, future play will be governed by an equilibrium that is unprofitable for it rather than by another one under which it would be profitable. While no such model has yet been developed, Pearce (1982) provides a discussion of the basic idea of early moves signalling which of several equilibria will obtain in subsequent play.

from their various choices. This will give them an incentive to try to learn the firm's costs; with this knowledge they can take the actions that will be optimal given what the firm will actually do, but without it the best they can do is optimize with respect to their prior beliefs about its costs and the actions it might take. If the firm could bias this learning, it could then hope to influence its rivals' behaviour to its benefit. In particular, if a firm's believing that its rival has low costs would induce it to exit or to limit its output, then the rival would want to foster the belief that its costs are low.

One avenue for attempting to learn the firm's costs is to try to infer them from its observed behaviour: the prices or quantities it chooses. Suppose that low costs are believed to be associated with low prices. Then, by setting lower prices than would otherwise be optimal, the firm can hope to bias its rivals' inferences, causing them to think that its costs are lower than they actually are, and thereby persuade them that it will be a tougher competitor than it actually would be. Further, since the firm's optimal choice absent this signalling/inference effect will be characterized by a zero-derivative condition, at the margin it is costless (to a first approximation) to shade the price. Thus, if its rivals are trying to infer costs from price, the firm will be led to try to influence their inferences and their resulting actions by setting its price low to signal low costs.

This 'signalling game' style of reasoning was first developed in Milgrom and Roberts (1982*a*), [16] where it was used to yield a theory of limit pricing: by biasing entrants' estimates of its costs downward, an incumbent can hope to reduce entry. It has also been used by Roberts (1986) to yield a theory of predation aimed at inducing exit or, failing that, restraining a rival's future output. [17] In this model, the predator is assumed to be better informed about demand conditions than is the prey, and its incentive is to make demand appear to be weak so that the prey will decide either that continued operations are not worth while or, at least, that if it does not exit it should produce the low quantities that are appropriate when demand is weak. Saloner (1987) has developed a model of

[16] Salop and Shapiro (1980) independently advanced a model of test-market predation based on the incumbent's private information about its costs. However, the restrictions they placed on the prices that could be chosen prevented their obtaining the full richness of the results that are inherent in the problem.

[17] This model in fact involves elements of both standard signalling models and signal jamming.

predation designed to soften up a merger candidate which also uses this logic: by convincing the target that it cannot compete profitably, the firm can hope to improve the terms upon which it makes the acquisition. Finally, Mailath (1984) has employed these methods to generate a model of price wars arising in situations where several firms have private information about pay-off-relevant variables.

Equilibrium in a signalling game of predation requires three conditions to hold: that, for each possible value of its private information, the predator choose the price or quantity that is optimal given its conjecture as to how the prey will react to each possible observed choice; that the prey act optimally, given its conjecture as to how the predator's observed choices depend on its private information; and that these conjectures about one another's strategies be correct. Thus, in equilibrium, no agent's beliefs can be systematically biased, even if some other agents are acting in ways that are intended to distort the agent's inferences. In equilibrium, agents will recognize the incentives that others face to alter their behaviour so as to influence inferences and will properly make allowances for these incentives in interpreting the behaviour that is observed. If the predator's equilibrium strategy results in observables that are a one-to-one function of its private information (a separating equilibrium), then in equilibrium the prey will correctly infer the predator's private information from its actions; if the strategy is not invertible, then a precise inference is not possible, but the prey will still be able to infer that the predator's information is such as to give rise to the particular realized observation, and this inference is not biased.

This rational expectations property of equilibrium has a striking implication: the predatory pricing that is generated in these theories does not cause its target to underestimate the profitability of continued operations or to overestimate the aggressiveness of the predator's future price and output choices. These depend on the predator's private information, of which the prey forms an unbiased estimate in equilibrium by making the appropriate inferences from its observations. Consequently, there is no reason to expect that the predation will induce exit or restrain rivals' future price and output choices by influencing inferences.[18]

[18] Of course, the recognition that the predator will attempt to bias inferences by setting lower prices or expanding output relative to what would otherwise be

This last point may seem paradoxical: if the predatory pricing is not going to succeed, why should it be practised? The reason is that the prey understand the incentives to try to influence their inferences, and in equilibrium they make allowances for these. Consequently, they interpret a particular observed level of price or output in light of the incentive to charge low prices, not as if there were no such incentive. As a result, if the potential predator were to deviate from its equilibrium behaviour and charge simply the (relatively high) price that would be appropriate if there were no incentive to try to influence beliefs, its rivals, seeing only this price, would interpret it as meaning that the firm has had higher costs than it actually does. They would then be even less likely to leave, and if they stay in, they would compete more aggressively, believing the firm to be relatively weak. The resulting extra competition means that the firm would be worse off than it would have been with the lower price corresponding to equilibrium behaviour.

The fact that this form of predation does not induce exit or discipline rivals might suggest that it is innocuous, or even socially beneficial if the resulting low prices are not too far below marginal costs. However, if the prospect of facing low profits due to predation by a better-informed, established firm deters entry (even though, should entry occur, the predation will not succeed), then the welfare implications of this form of predation are ambiguous.[19] Thus, there may be some interest in considering the circumstances under which it might be expected.

The first key assumption in these models is that one of the firms, the potential predator, is better informed than the other about a variable, such as demand or costs, whose value is relevant for the latter's decisions. Such an assumption would often seem plausible if the second firm is a recent or potential entrant, if the predator has just introduced a new version of the product, or if it has opened new production facilities or adopted a new technology with which the prey is not familiar. A change in management or ownership of the predator might also suffice if it might be associated with a shift in objectives or strategy. Finally, if market conditions are changing and the one firm is known to have better market research or to have

optimal will influence the prey's price and output choices during the predatory episode. See Roberts (1986).

[19] This possibility was noted by Scharfstein (1984).

access to information from other markets with which it is familiar, then the informational asymmetry assumption might again be expected to hold. To the extent that these latter characteristics are likely to be positively associated with size or multimarket operations, the traditional view of which sort of firm is likely to be the predator is supported. Of course, the better-informed firm might also be a new entrant with costs that are unobservable by the established firms.

Secondly, these models assume that there is no effective way that the better-informed firm can make its information available to the other firms directly and credibly; otherwise, given the nature of equilibrium in these models, it would do so.[20] In this context, the models usually assume that the private information is about a simple, one-dimensional variable, because this assumption greatly simplifies the formal analysis.[21] It might, on the surface, seem fairly simple to reveal such information directly: for example, perhaps the firm could bring in outsiders to observe its operations to see that its costs are not higher than it claims. Yet, in reality, it might prove very difficult to transmit credibly something like an estimate of demand, even if it were a single number, and when the private information is more complex, it might be impossible to remove the asymmetry.

A third assumption is needed in the formal model to generate predation. It is that the less-informed firm will actually attempt to infer the better-informed firm's private information from its price and output decisions and that the informed firm will recognize this and attempt to take advantage of it. Also, for the conclusion that the low prices will not distort the exit decision, it is also necessary that the prey correctly interpret the informed firm's choices in terms of its incentives. While there is some empirical and experimental support for signalling models that would suggest that at least the first two of these are not totally implausible, as we will see below, they are not strictly necessary: other formulations will generate

---

[20] It might seem that, for some values of its private information, the firm would not want it revealed. For example, if the equilibrium strategy pools firms with different cost levels, then high-cost firms may benefit from being pooled with those with low costs. However, the low-cost firms would freely reveal their costs if it were possible, because they would gain from being recognized as tough competitors. Thus, failure to reveal would indicate high costs. See Milgrom and Roberts (1986).

[21] Indeed, the study of multidimensional signalling is at a very early stage, and there have been few applications.

similar behaviour. Of course, if one accepts the first two assumptions and not the third, then the predation will induce exit, and it then becomes more of a matter for antitrust concern. For example, attempts to disrupt an entrant's test marketing could succeed in deterring a producer from committing itself to the whole market when the incumbent knows that it would be profitable.

Finally, although most of the models in this vein deal with only a single predator and prey, this is not crucial. In fact, demonstration effects are easily formalized in this work, and having several markets to protect can be expected to increase the incentives for predation in any one.

In any case, if one is inclined to worry about this form of predation as an antitrust issue, then it is important to recognize that the predatory prices that it generates need bear no direct relation to the predator's marginal cost. To induce exit, all that is needed is that the price should, in the long run, be expected to be below the prey's average avoidable costs—essentially, long-run average costs. And to limit future output from the prey, the predator need only convince the prey that its costs are lower than they actually are; this need not even involve prices below average costs.[22] Thus, even when the two firms have the same costs, the Areeda–Turner test would not necessarily identify this pricing as predatory. Meanwhile, if the predator faces lower costs—for example, if the issue is whether the prey should incur the costs involved in entering a previously uncontested market—then the predatory prices might well be above the predator's current average cost.

Thus, the signalling models of predation cause real problems for the conclusions of orthodox analysis. The same is true for the models based on signal jamming or reputations.

The signal-jamming approach is formally somewhat different from the signalling one in that it relies on different sorts of informational asymmetries, but it is very similar in spirit and in the conclusions it yields. The one well-developed signal-jamming model of predation is due to Fudenberg and Tirole (1986), but an earlier contribution using this logic is Riordan's (1985) model of price wars.

The essence of signal jamming is that there is again a variable that is not directly observable and whose value the prey is trying to

---

[22] This assumes something like Cournot competition, where equilibrium market shares are negatively related to costs.

learn because it is relevant to its future profits and thus to its price, quantity, and exit decisions. Again too, the distribution of the observable correlates of the underlying variable of interest are assumed to depend on the actions of the potential predator. Thus, the predator can hope to bias the inferences drawn by the prey by altering its own actions. However, in this set-up, there is no assumption that the predator is better informed about the variable's true value. Thus, its actions cannot depend on the value of the variable, as they do in standard signalling models. Nevertheless, there is an asymmetry of information: it is assumed that the actions of the predator that influence the values of the observed variables are themselves not observed by the prey. (Otherwise, the prey could simply net them out and there would be no possibility of influencing its inferences.) There is also a necessity of assuming an asymmetry of position between the firms which in some ways parallels the asymmetry in the signalling models of assuming that one firm is informed and the other not. Specifically, one of the firms must be assumed to be entertaining a decision to exit. This firm becomes the prey. If both were willing to consider exiting, then one would get a model of price wars, not of predation.

A context in which this sort of theory might be particularly applicable is one where the prey is test-marketing a product in a market where the predator is already active. Here the asymmetry of position and the unobservability of actions seem reasonable. By offering *sub rosa* price breaks to distributors, utilizing coupons, increasing promotions, etc., the established firm can hope to disrupt the prey's test, cause it to underestimate the profitability of its product, and thereby discourage it from entering fully.

The properties of equilibrium in signal-jamming models are essentially those with signalling. The predator cuts price to bias the prey's inferences; the prey allows for this behaviour and so is not fooled; consequently there is no effect on exit or on future price-output decisions; and yet there may be some deterrence of entry by the threat of predation, even though, should the entry occur, the predation will be 'unsuccessful'. Again too, there need be no connection between the predatory prices and marginal or average variable costs, so the relevance of the Areeda–Turner test is problematic.

A striking feature of these first two types of theories is that although the predator is aiming at driving out or disciplining a current rival, it fails to do so, and yet the rational expectation that it will attempt to prey in order to influence inferences may deter entry. In the third class of predation models—those based on reputation arguments—the objective is explicitly to deter future entry by preying on current rivals, independent of whether the predation induces its target to exit.

The first formal reputation models of predation were developed by Kreps and Wilson (1982) and Milgrom and Roberts (1982*b*). In these models, a firm operating (or anticipating operating) in several markets preys on any early entrants, even if it is not worth while to do so in terms of the profits that are received from the entered market alone. This predation is practised in order to develop a 'reputation for toughness' that deters other potential entrants because it leads them to expect that their entry will meet the same predatory response.

The analysis depends on an informational asymmetry of the type used in the signalling models: it is private information to the predator whether it would prey in a single market absent any demonstration effects.[23] Such a willingness to prey might arise from cost considerations directly, from contracts written between owners and management that reward sales instead of profits (see Fershtman and Judd 1987), or simply from a streak of craziness. The key point is that failure to prey against a single rival implies that the incumbent is not a 'natural' predator that would fight all attempts at entry. Then, future entrants need not fear predation at all, and so all will enter.[24] In contrast, preying keeps alive the possibility that future entrants will also meet an aggressive response and, if this possibility is sufficiently unattractive to these entrants, they may be deterred. Thus, preying may be worth while, even though it is immediately costly. In fact, if a sufficient number of

[23] If there were an infinite number of markets—as might be the case if the markets were for different generations of a firm's products—then there is no need for an informational asymmetry to generate predation for reputation. However, in such contexts there will also be many non-predatory equilibria. See Roberts (1987) and Ordover and Saloner 1987.

[24] With a fixed, finite number of potential entrants, if it is common knowledge that the incumbent would not prey against a single entrant in isolation, then in the only subgame perfect equilibrium all the potential entrants do enter and the incumbent never preys. The logic is by induction. The incumbent will not prey if the last entrant comes in, and thus entry will occur at the last stage, independent of the history at previous rounds. But since preying against the second-last entrant cannot deter entry by the last one, the incumbent will not prey at the next-to-last stage, and so entry occurs then too. But now the logic applies at the third-to-last stage.

markets remain to protect, the probability that the entrants ascribe to the incumbent being a natural predator can be made arbitrarily small, and predation will still be the response to entry: although the firm actually finds predation unprofitable in isolation, it will fight if challenged, mimicking the behaviour of the natural predator, in order to maintain its reputation for toughness and deter future entry. Of course, the anticipation that the firm will fight to protect its reputation in itself serves to deter current entry attempts as well.

Easley, Masson, and Reynolds (1985) have also developed a reputation model of predation by a firm operating in a number of markets. The profitability of entry into any of these markets is unknown to the potential entrants, but it is known to be correlated across markets. Demand may possibly be low, in which case entry is unattractive, but if it is high, then entry is warranted. In equilibrium, if demand actually is strong the incumbent unobservably cuts price (as in the signal-jamming model) to generate observables that mimic those when demand is weak. It thereby develops a reputation for weakness of demand in its markets that deters or delays further entry.

These sorts of model would seem most applicable when there is a firm operating in numerous markets where what happens in one market is both observable to participants in other markets and reasonably considered as being indicative of what would happen in these other markets in similar circumstances. These markets could be geographical ones, they could be for different products at any given time, or they could be defined over time. The more such markets there are to protect—the greater are the incentives to build and maintain a reputation that deters challenges. Thus, in particular, the high-tech industries would seem particularly suited to generating such pricing.

In signalling and signal-jamming stories, predation was not socially undesirable once entry occurred, and its only negative effect was the essentially unintended one on entry. In some contrast, in the present set-up, if entry does occur then its being met by predation strengthens the predator's reputation and has a further deterrent effect. Thus, this sort of predation seems more troubling from an antitrust viewpoint. However, again it is the case that predation need not drive its target out of business to be effective, nor is it necessary to impose operating losses: it is enough that profits be sufficiently small or delayed that they do not justify sinking the costs of entry. Again, the Areeda–Turner test is irrelevant.

4. Thoughts on Policy Implications

Traditional economic theory questions whether predation is likely to occur, and suggests that prohibitions aimed at it will be efficiency-reducing, deterring normal competitive behaviour. Despite this, business people, lawyers, industrial organization scholars, legislators, and courts have treated predation both as a real occurrence and as a problem. However, the litigation of predation has had a tendency to get into messy, expensive and ambiguous determinations of intent. At least in the United States, the response to the resulting inefficiences—both in the costs of trial and in the effects on business of being unsure of the legality of various practices—has been to attempt to lay down sharp rules for behaviour, principally defining illegal predation to be the setting of prices below some measure of costs. Of course this approach does not address the lack of an economic theory generating predation.

The more recent economic analyses discussed here suggest that firms will, in fact, attempt to exclude rivals by setting lower prices than they would find optimal if there was no hope of inducing exit, deterring entry, or persuading rivals to accept limited market shares. We have called such behaviour 'predatory', because both its form and its intent match the traditional use of this term. Yet, as we have accentuated above, it need not involve prices that are low enough to run foul of the proposed tests for predation. Moreover, a pure monopolist unconcerned with actual or potential competitors but employing a technology with strong learning effects could rationally price below (current) marginal cost. Thus, price levels that the tests would label as predatory need not be such in fact. Consequently, it would seem that there is little value to these tests. Moreover, these same failures seem sure to haunt any other attempt at a simple mechanical rule.

Beyond this, of course, is the issue of whether antitrust law ought to attack prices that are predatory in the sense used here. We have seen that this behaviour can be socially costly, not in the expected fashion of eliminating current competition but rather through an impact on future entry. Thus, could it be clearly identified and effectively prohibited, there might be gains to doing so. But this would involve requiring firms to charge the 'right' prices—those that they would charge if the market and informational conditions gave no possibility of affecting rivals' behaviour![25] The problems of determining what these prices are are mind-boggling. Doing so would surely cost more than any efficiency gain one might realize from reducing the height of dead-weight-loss triangles. And, given the complexity of actual business decisions and the subtle nature of the behaviour and inferences involved, it is not at all clear that even determining intent can work, no matter what the costs incurred. If so, it may be best simply to give up on attempts to control predation, even if one believes that it can and does occur.

[25] This is in essence what is called for in the predation test proposed by Ordover and Willig (1981).

References

Abruzzese, L. (1987), 'Study Finds Evidence of Predatory Pricing', *Journal of Commerce*, 17 June 1987, 2.

Areeda, P. E. and Turner, D. F. (1975), 'Predatory Pricing and Related Practices under Section 2 of the Sherman Act', *Harvard Law Review*, 88: 697–733.

Benoit, J.-P. (1984), 'Financially Constrained Entry in a Game with Incomplete Information', *Rand Journal of Economics*, 15: 490–9.

Bolton, P. and Scharfstein, D. (1988), 'Agency Problems, Financial Contracting, and Predation', Working Paper 1986–8, Sloan School of Management, MIT.

Burns, M. (1986), 'Predatory Pricing and the Acquisition Cost of Competitors', *Journal of Political Economy*, 94: 266–96.

—— (1987), 'Empirical Studies of Predatory Price Cutting: Second Thoughts and New Evidence', mimeo., Dept. of Economics, University of Kansas.

Easley, D., Masson, R. and Reynolds, R. (1985), 'Preying for Time', *International Journal of Industrial Organization*, 33: 445–60.

Farrell, J. and Saloner, G. (1986), 'Installed Base and Compatibility: Innovation, Product Preannouncements, and Predation', *American Economic Review*, 76: 940–55.

Fershtman, C. and Judd, K. (1987), 'Equilibrium Incentives in Oligopoly', *American Economic Review*, 77: 927–40.

Fudenberg, D. and Tirole, J. (1983), 'Learning by Doing and Market Performance', *Bell Journal of Economics*, 14: 522–30.

—— and —— (1985), 'Predation without Reputation', Working Paper 377, Dept. of Economics, MIT.

—— and —— (1986), 'A "Signal-Jamming" Theory of Predation', *Rand Journal of Economics*, 17: 366–77.

Gale, D. and Hellwig, M. (1985), 'Incentive Compatible Debt Contracts: The One-Period Problem', *Review of Economic Studies*, 52: 647–64.

Katz, M. and Shapiro, C. (1986), 'Technology Adoption in the Presence of Network Externalities', *Journal of Political Economy*, 94: 822–41.

Klemperer, P. (1986), *Markets with Consumer Switching Costs*, Ph.D. thesis, Graduate School of Business, Stanford University.

Kreps, D. and Wilson, R. (1982), 'Reputation and Imperfect Information', *Journal of Economic Theory*, 27: 253–79.

McGee, J. (1958), 'Predatory Price Cutting: The Standard Oil (N.J.) Case', *Journal of Law and Economics*, 1: 137–69.

—— (1980), 'Predatory Pricing Revisited', *Journal of Law and Economics*, 23: 289–330.

Mailath, G. (1984), 'The Welfare Implications of Differential Information in a Dynamic Duopoly Model', mimeo., Dept. of Economics, Princeton University.

Milgrom, P. (1987), 'Predatory Pricing', in J. Eatwell, M. Milgate, and P. Newman (eds.), *The New Palgrave, A Dictionary of Economics*, Stockton Press, New York, iii. 937–8.

—— and Roberts, J. (1982*a*), 'Limit Pricing and Entry under Incomplete Information: An Equilibrium Analysis', *Econometrica*, 50: 443–59.

—— and —— (1982*b*), 'Predation, Reputation and Entry Deterrence', *Journal of Economic Theory*, 27: 280–312.

—— and —— (1986), 'Relying on the Information of Interested Parties', *Rand Journal of Economics*, 17: 18–32.

—— and —— (1987), 'Informational Asymmetries, Strategic Behaviour, and Industrial Organization', *American Economic Review, Papers and Proceedings*, 77: 184–93.

Ordover, J. A. and Willig, R. (1981), 'An Economic Definition of Predation: Pricing and Product Innovation', *Yale Law Journal*, 91: 8–53.

Ordover, J. A. and Saloner, G. (1987), 'Predation, Monopolization and Antitrust', Working Paper E-87-17, Domestic Studies Program, Hoover Institution, Stanford University. (To appear in R. Schmalensee and R. Willig (eds.), *Handbook of Industrial Organization*, North-Holland, Amsterdam, 1989.

Pearce, D. (1982), 'A Problem with Single-Valued Solution Concepts', mimeo., Dept. of Economics, Princeton University.

Posner, R. (1976), *Antitrust Law: An Economic Perspective*, University of Chicago Press, Chicago, Ill.

Riordan, M. (1985), 'Imperfect Information and Dynamic Conjectural Variations', *Rand Journal of Economics*, 16: 41–50.

Roberts, J. (1986), 'A Signalling Model of Predatory Pricing', *Oxford Economic Papers*, 38: 75–93 (supplement).

—— (1987), 'Battles for Market Share: Incomplete Information, Aggressive Strategic Pricing and Competitive Dynamics', in T. Bewley (ed.), *Advances in Economic Theory*, Cambridge University Press, Cambridge, 157–95.

Saloner, G. (1987), 'Predation, Mergers, and Incomplete Information', *Rand Journal of Economics*, 18: 165–86.

Salop, S. and Shapiro, C. (1980), 'A Guide to Test Market Predation', (unpub.).

Scharfstein, D. (1984), 'A Policy to Prevent Rational Test-Marketing Predation', *Rand Journal of Economics*, 15: 229–43.

Scherer, F. M. (1970), *Industrial Market Structure and Economic Performance*, Rand McNally, Chicago, Ill.

Telser, L. (1966), 'Cutthroat Competition and the Long Purse', *Journal of Law and Economics*, 9: 259–77.

Townsend, R. (1979), 'Optimal Contracts and Competitive Markets with Costly State Verification', *Journal of Economic Theory*, 21: 265–93.

Yamey, B. (1972), 'Predatory Price Cutting: Notes and Comments', *Journal of Law and Economics*, 15: 129–42.

7

Empirical Studies of Rivalrous Behaviour

Richard Schmalensee

The landscape of industrial organization, particularly in the United States, was for many years dominated by a bitter struggle between Harvard and Chicago. Chicago's partisans assumed that rivalry would generally be intense in the absence of government regulation or effective cartel arrangements. They accordingly relied on the price theory of Alfred Marshall and, for the cartel case, Joan Robinson. Harvard's loyalists, on the other hand, assumed that competition was often seriously imperfect even in the absence of regulation or cartels. They tended to employ less-formal analytical frameworks derived from the works of Edward Chamberlin and William Fellner.

The differences in the dialects of economics spoken by the two schools were such that debates about scientific issues often seemed in need of translators.[1] Empirical work by each school tended to support its basic assumption about market conduct. Policy prescriptions also reflected those assumptions. Harvard called for an activist government policy to deal with serious imperfections in competition, while Chicago, believing that such imperfections were rare, argued for *laissez-faire*.

In the last two decades the study of industrial organization has been transformed by rigorous theoretical analyses of imperfect competition. Graduate courses in industrial organization now cover a host of sophisticated, game-theoretic models of imperfect competition, some of which have been reviewed in the other chapters in this volume.[2] There are no deep divisions or distinct schools in this domain; broadly similar theoretical papers are written and studied at Harvard, Chicago, and other leading institutions in the United States and abroad. The dialect of game theory is spoken everywhere.

[1] Perhaps the clearest examples of adherents of the two schools shouting past each other can be found in Goldschmid, Mann, and Weston 1974.

[2] Tirole 1988 provides a superb general outline of the theoretical literature in industrial organization.

One might expect that this convergence in theoretical method and the development of a large and widely studied body of theoretical literature would have served to narrow differences in the empirical and policy domains. But this does not seem to have happened. Methods and assumptions employed in empirical work seem if anything more diverse than two decades ago, and the controversies about basic factual questions that raged then continue largely unabated now. And, even though distinct Harvard and Chicago Schools are no longer present in the theoretical literature, defenders of their traditional positions still dominate many policy debates.

In the remainder of this chapter I consider causes and potential cures for this fragmentation on matters of substance, concentrating on the actual and potential contribution of empirical studies of rivalrous behaviour in real markets.[3] In the next section I argue that theoretical work in industrial organization has, somewhat paradoxically, made it clear that empirical research is absolutely critical to progress in this field. The current fragmentation of the field reflects in large measure the loss of faith in the two approaches to empirical research—comprehensive industry case studies and cross-section industry-level profitability studies—that dominated empirical work in industrial organization until roughly the start of this decade. These approaches are discussed in sections 2 and 3, respectively.

The 1980s have witnessed what Tim Bresnahan and I (Bresnahan and Schmalensee 1987) have been incautious enough to call an empirical renaissance in industrial economics. Compared with the earlier literature, recent research is notable for its methodological diversity. Sections 4 and 5 discuss some particularly promising approaches to industry-specific and inter-industry studies, respectively, that figure prominently in recent work. Though the organization of sections 2–5 highlights methods used rather than questions addressed, important empirical findings and problems are discussed as well. Section 6 briefly summarizes some of the main themes that emerge from this overview and offers some modest prescriptions.

---

[3] I thus resist the temptation to discuss the emerging literature on laboratory experiments in industrial organization; see Plott 1988 for a comprehensive survey.

1. Theory and Empirics

Industrial organization is primarily concerned with the behaviour of business firms in their roles as sellers and with the implications of that behaviour for the operation of markets and the design of public policy. While game-theoretic tools are well-suited in principle to the analysis of key aspects of business behaviour, their application has neither produced a general theory of market operation nor given one much reason to expect such a theory to emerge in the foreseeable future. Under these conditions, empirical research becomes critical to scientific progress.

The Nature of Recent Theorizing

Game theory was developed in large part to model rational behaviour in small-numbers situations, and many industrial markets have only a few important sellers. Indeed, in retrospect, the only surprise is that game theory took forty years to conquer oligopoly theory. But there is more to the appeal of game theory than this.

Many important aspects of business conduct are inherently dynamic. Actions and reactions take time; productive assets are often long-lived; entry and exit decisions turn on 'before' and 'after' comparisons. In addition, information in real markets is rarely complete, perfect, or symmetric. Potential entrants may know less about a market than established firms, for instance, and individual established firms may know only their own costs, not those of their rivals. Recent advances in extensive form game theory have greatly facilitated the analysis of situations that involve strategic behaviour over time in settings in which information is incomplete and asymmetric. There is no comparably attractive approach to the analysis of such situations anywhere in sight.

Unfortunately, however, the general impression that has emerged from a decade's extensive use of the game-theoretic approach is 'Anything can happen!' The diversity and growth of the theoretical literature provides a good deal of support for the conjecture that almost any remotely plausible pattern of conduct—anything that has ever been alleged with a straight face in an antitrust case, say— can appear in an equilibrium in an apparently plausible game-theoretic model. Policy implications are in some sense even more varied, since efficient policy in many models depends on details of parameter values and functional forms.

This situation flows from two apparently general features of game-theoretic models of market behaviour.[4] The first is that many apparently simple multiperiod games of incomplete information have multiple equilibria—often an uncountable infinity of equilibria. Though considerable work has been done to refine the definition of equilibrium in order to mitigate this problem, it still remains endemic. Current practice often involves selecting a single equilibrium on the basis of model-specific plausibility arguments. Sometimes these arguments are compelling; in other cases 'anything can happen' is the only way to summarize the multitude of a single model's equilibria.

Even game-theoretic models that have unique equilibria possess a second feature that is in some respects even more troubling: the predictions of game-theoretic models seem delicate and are often difficult to test. Important qualitative features of equilibria often depend critically on whether prices or quantities are choice variables, on whether discrete or continuous time is assumed, on whether moves are sequential or simultaneous, and, perhaps most disturbing of all, on how players with incomplete information are assumed to alter their beliefs in response to events that do not occur in equilibrium. When information is incomplete, strategies depend on unobservable beliefs, and the often empirically questionable assumption that key parameters and probability distributions are common knowledge is frequently central to the analysis. The level of rationality required of actors in many game-theoretic models seems to exceed the capabilities of all but the best economic theorists.

Thus, game-theoretic modelling has taught us a great deal about what *might* happen in a variety of situations, but relatively little about what *must* happen conditional on observables. Game theory has proven better at generating internally consistent scenarios than at providing plausible and testable restrictions on real behaviour. It seems almost certain that the theoretical literature contains a sizeable number of what Clapham (1922) called 'empty boxes'— internally consistent models that describe no real markets—and that more such boxes are being constructed daily. But there is no

---

[4] This paragraph and the next have been heavily influenced by Fudenberg and Tirole 1987 and Milgrom and Roberts 1987.

consensus on which models belong to this class and which others should be taken particularly seriously because their predictions are often correct. Thus, disputes about issues of fact and policy can and do flourish despite an impressive array of theoretical results and insights.

Moreover, the very diversity of predictions in the theoretical literature seems to cast doubt on the value of theory in this field. The sensitivity of equilibrium outcomes to modelling details seems to suggest that one must know more than anyone is likely ever to know about any real market in order to use theory to make definite predictions about conduct and performance.

The Roles of Empirical Research

Absent a theoretical breakthrough, it seems clear that only empirical research can alter this state of affairs, since only empirical testing can definitively establish the domain of applicability of any model. This is the most-cited role of empirical research in this or any field: testing theories in a variety of settings to see under what conditions, if any, their predictions are valid. Because most of the theoretical literature in industrial organization remains untested in this sense, theorists are free to generalize, extend, innovate, and explore with essentially no external constraints.

Game-theoretic models are particularly hard to test, since their predictions are sensitive to market details it is often difficult or (in the case of models in which beliefs and expectations play a critical role) impossible to observe. But, as Friedman (1953) stressed, predictions are ultimately what matters. That is, in situations in which a model's assumptions are at least plausible (Friedman might argue against this condition), one can concentrate on confronting its predictions with the facts. The domain of any model's applicability can then be determined by analysis of the similarities and differences between and among situations in which it does and does not perform well.

While most general discussions of empirical research stress theory testing, such research also has two other critical roles to play in industrial organization. The first is simply to provide facts with which theories must be consistent. Tests that reject widely accepted theories or indicate that they have a narrow range of validity yield such facts automatically, of course. But empirical studies not primarily aimed at theory testing may also play this role. Early astronomers aimed simply to describe the heavens; their results on the movements of the planets provided key facts in the development of theories of gravitation.

Unfortunately, few theories are ever conclusively rejected in economics. And the low value placed on descriptive research by much of the economics profession depresses the volume of such research. Industrial-organization theorists thus confront a relatively small fact base and are free to build models that relate to no well-described real market, since few markets are in fact well described.

The third role of empirical research in industrial organization is to inform the analysis of particular industries and the design of general policy rules by providing information on the frequency with which particular market structures and patterns of conduct occur in the economy. If, for instance, predatory pricing never occurs, the ideal policy is to ignore charges of predation, since any other policy can only waste resources. This is in many respects the hardest of the three roles. We have concentration ratios for most manufacturing markets in many economies, for instance, but little comprehensive information is available on more subtle aspects of market structure, and essentially no systematic data aside from accounting profit rates is available on conduct or performance. This leaves a factual vacuum in policy debates that is quickly filled by beliefs and assumptions.

2.   Classical Industry Case Studies

Industry-level case studies were central to the research programme of the Harvard School when it emerged under the leadership of Edward Mason and others in the 1930s. Lacking a satisfactory theory of business behaviour in concentrated, dynamic markets with incomplete information, these scholars initially hoped to develop useful generalizations inductively by carefully examining structure, conduct, and performance in many markets. These examinations tended to be reported in comprehensive, book-length studies; see Wallace 1937 for an early and influential study of the aluminium industry and Peck 1961 for an interesting follow-up.

These studies tended to be qualitative and historical in nature and to emphasize the evolution of market structure and patterns of behaviour over time. Since such work required both broad and deep information, case studies written in the United States often relied on data and documents collected and made public in the course of antitrust cases. Thus, concentrated industries that seemed, at least to antitrust authorities, to behave non-competitively tended to be over-represented in the case-study literature.

The best of these early industry studies summarized mountains of documents and testimony into a consistent and generally persuasive picture. They regularly described patterns of conduct that were not easily explained by simple competitive or monopoly models. Studies of the inter-war United States cigarette industry by Tennant (1950) and Nicholls (1951), for instance, found an early period of differing and frequently changed prices, followed by a long period of price leadership, during which list prices were identical and only rarely changed.[5] Rivalry apparently shifted to advertising and away from price early in this second period.[6]

This single data point was highly influential. It showed clearly the limits of both competitive and monopoly models, and it drew attention to the phenomena of price leadership, price rigidity, and shifts from price to non-price rivalry as industries matured. In addition to specific observations of this sort, classical case studies helped to shape the world views of several generations of scholars by providing a wealth of detailed qualitative information about business decision-making and its effects.

The production of high-quality comprehensive industry studies seems to have peaked around 1960. It may have become increasingly clear that the Harvard School's inductive research programme, like recent theoretical research, was better at generating interesting examples and observations than useful general rules. Moreover, comprehensive case studies were time-consuming, often involved a great deal of subjective judgement, and tended to cover only a small, non-representative sample of industries for which usually private data had been made public. Systematic comparative evaluations of case studies were difficult because the individual

[5] An earlier study by Cox (1933) is much less informative—largely, I think, because Cox did not have available the antitrust trial record on which Tennant and Nicholls relied heavily.

[6] This pattern of conduct persisted after World War II, and product innovation became an important form of non-price rivalry. See Schmalensee (1972: 125–33) for a brief discussion of the early post-war period.

studies were not easily summarized. And an alternative approach had become increasingly attractive.

3.   Classical Cross-Section Studies

Joe Bain's (1951, 1956) seminal inter-industry cross-section profitability studies were based on the deceptively simple observation that the effective exercise of monopoly power should on average yield monopoly profits. The statistical analysis of profitability differences among large samples of markets thus seemed to promise rapid and objective development of general relationships regarding the incidence of monopolistic behaviour.

Bain's own work was marked by extremely careful development of quantitative data based on detailed qualitative knowledge of the markets in his samples. Perhaps because few could confidently imitate this style or because multiple regression analysis was not routine in the 1950s, few scholars followed Bain's lead initially. But, as computation costs fell and government-supplied industry-level data became more widely available, the journals began to fill with cross-section profitability studies in the 1960s, and the production of comprehensive industry studies waned.

Much cross-section research focused on Bain's (1951) original hypothesis: effective collusion, and thus supra-competitive profitability, are more likely when concentration is high. Over time, more effort was devoted to following Bain's (1956) later work and considering the effects of entry conditions.[7] Most early studies tended to support the existence of a positive relation between concentration and profitability, though that relation was often statistically fragile and economically weak. And a number of variables that arguably proxied for the difficulty of entry were also positively related to profitability; some of these relations (notably that involving the advertising-sales ratio) were quite robust.

But during the 1970s critics of this general approach became vocal and persuasive, and a number of empirical anomalies were uncovered. As a result, relatively few scholars at the start of this decade believed that the industry-level cross-section literature had

---

[7] A number of the points made in the remainder of this section and in s. 5 are discussed in more detail and with more complete references to the literature in Schmalensee 1988.

shed much light on the structural determinants of non-competitive behaviour.

Measurement Problems

The design of Bain's (1951) original study and many that followed involved comparing seller profitability and concentration in a sample of manufacturing markets. The first critics of this approach argued that neither concentration nor profitability could be observed accurately in practice. As the specifications of cross-section models became more complex and as the theoretical literature developed, additional measurement problems became apparent.

Bain had first to decide what collections of products and regions for which data were available constituted economic markets. This is often not a simple task even when detailed data are available, as any antitrust veteran will testify. Then Bain had to decide how to measure concentration. He chose the total market share of the eight largest sellers, which later work has shown to be highly, though not perfectly, correlated with alternative plausible measures.

Finally, Bain had to decide how to measure seller profitability. He chose to use the average ratio of accounting profits to the balance-sheet value of net worth (or owners' equity) for the firms in each market for which he was able to collect data. Unfortunately, it is by now well known that accounting measures of the rate of return on assets or net worth are at best noisy measures of firms' true, economic rates of return. Conventional accounting systems treat inflation and depreciation improperly (Fisher and McGowan 1983), and accounting practices vary among firms and over time.

Some authors have sought to avoid capital-related accounting biases by using the so-called price-cost margin (revenue − labour and materials cost)/revenue. But this measure has little theoretical or empirical support (Liebowitz 1982); radically different values of the price-cost margin can yield identical rates of return on owners' investment when capital intensities differ. Recently, a number of authors have used Tobin's q, the ratio of a firm's market value to the replacement cost of its assets, as a measure of profitability (Salinger 1984). But the measurement of replacement cost inevitably relies critically on accounting data.

Even if accounting data were not inherently noisy, most large modern firms sell in multiple markets and have assets and expenses that are not easily allocated among those markets. Even though his data were from the 1930s, when diversification was less of a problem than today, Bain was thus required to define some of his markets broadly (e.g. aluminium products) so as to include most of his firms' revenues. Today, firm-level data are rarely used for market-orientated cross-section studies unless product-mix information can be used to construct weighted averages of the features of the markets in which each firm sells.

Many cross-section profitability studies attempt to avoid the diversification problem by using data for individual plants or business units. Since plants' outputs are typically more homogeneous than firms', it is more frequently plausible to assign plants to particular markets than to assign entire firms. But data derived in this fashion, like those in the United States Census of Manufactures, omit costs that are not incurred at the plant level and tend to force the use of measures, like the price-cost margin, that ignore capital costs. The obvious alternative is to use data in which firms themselves have allocated costs to each of the markets from which they receive revenue; the United States Federal Trade Commission's Line of Business data (Ravenscraft 1983) and the PIMS data set of the Strategic Planning Institute provide frequently employed examples. The obvious danger here is that cost allocations are inevitably somewhat arbitrary.

Early defenders of the cross-section approach (e.g. Weiss 1971) had a ready reply to attacks based on measurement error. They noted that as long as measurement errors are random, they tend to mask true relations, not exaggerate them. Thus, rather than indicting the whole cross-section approach, measurement errors provide an excuse for the weak results it frequently produces.

But the argument does not end there. Random measurement errors should cause the variance of accounting rates of return to exceed that of real, economic rates of return. And a number of authors (e.g. Alberts (1984) and Salinger (1984)) have observed that differences among accounting measures of firm profitability in the United States are generally too small to be easily reconciled with the existence of much monopoly power in the economy, even if measurement error is assumed away.[8] That is, even if accounting

[8] This is basically why studies of the aggregate welfare costs of monopoly power that follow Harberger 1954 and base their analysis on differences in profit rates tend to find small costs.

profit measures were exact and perfectly correlated with concentration, the estimated effect of concentration on market performance would be small. The real effect, if any, must be even smaller because of measurement error.

Data on after-tax returns on equity from Bain's (1951) original study illustrate this point nicely. Suppose the competitive value of this measure of profitability is r_c. Then if r is the after-tax rate of return on equity for some firm exercising monopoly power, we must have:

$$(1) \quad r - r_c = \frac{(1 - \tau)\,(R - C)}{E} = \left[\frac{(1 - \tau)R}{E} \right] \left[\frac{R - C}{R} \right],$$

where τ is the corporate tax rate, R is revenue, C is total cost (including normal profit), and E is owners' equity. A plausible estimate of r_c is the average after-tax rate of return on equity in Bain's twenty unconcentrated industries: 6.9 per cent. It appears that $[(1 - \tau)R/E]$ averages about 1.12 for the firms in Bain's sample.[9] Thus, an observed r of 16 per cent corresponds to a mark-up over total cost $[(R - C)/R]$ of about 8.1 per cent $[16.0 - 6.9)/1.12]$, which would be chosen by a monopoly facing a demand elasticity of about 12. Such a high demand elasticity implies little monopoly power, yet only three of Bain's twenty-two concentrated industries had r's above 16 per cent.

Bain's data also illustrate the general weakness of estimated concentration/profitability relations. Using this same approach, the average r in his preferred sample of concentrated industries corresponds to a demand elasticity of about 22. For other samples (see his Table 3), implied elasticities range from 31 to 111, and the corresponding profitability differences are generally insignificant.

Studies that went beyond concentration to consider conditions of entry encountred yet another layer of measurement problems. Bain (1956) performed small-scale case studies for each industry in his sample and assessed barriers to entry judgementally. Since entry will eliminate excess profits in the absence of barriers, Bain tested—and found some support for—an interactive hypothesis: profits are high only when both concentration and barriers to entry are high.

[9] This number was derived from US Internal Revenue Service, *Statistics of Income* for 1938, the middle year in Bain's sample.

Later authors generally eschewed both Bain's labour-intensive and inherently subjective measurement approach and his theoretically plausible interactive specification.[10] Following the influential work of Comanor and Wilson (1967), most studies employed additive regression models in which both concentration and proxies for entry barriers appear as independent variables. Not only are additive specifications suspect on a priori grounds, but it is unclear that commonly employed proxies, such as the market share of a medium-sized plant and the advertising/sales ratio, measure conditions of entry at all well. The theoretical literature suggests that other factors that are more resistant to measurement, such as information structures and the extent to which costs are sunk, are at least as important as scale economies. And the theoretical link between the advertising intensities of established firms, which clearly depend heavily on difficult-to-quantify features of the product involved, and entry conditions is tenuous at best.

It is perhaps not surprising in light of the discussion of Bain (1951) above that when variables intended to proxy for conditions of entry and other elements of market structure are added to cross-section profitability regressions, the coefficient of concentration is often negative or insignificant (e.g. Comanor and Wilson 1967, Porter 1976).

Identification Problems

A later and ultimately more potent stream of criticism began with Demsetz's (1973) argument that profitability and concentration could be positively correlated in cross-section even if concentration had no effect on the intensity of rivalry. His argument relied on inter-firm differences and pointed towards the endogeneity of concentration, two key themes in much recent research.

Since the standard presumption is that cross-section studies aim to reveal differences among long-run equilibria, Demsetz's argument is most naturally illustrated in that context.[11] It is then plausible to let quantity (which one can think of as capacity) be the strategic variable and assume constant returns to scale. Thus,

---

[10] Tests of interactive specifications were performed by a few later authors (see e.g. Caves, Porter, and Spence 1980 and Salinger 1984) and produced generally negative results.

[11] This development follows Schmalensee 1987a; see also Cowling and Waterson 1976 and Clarke, Davies, and Waterson 1984.

consider a homogeneous-product industry in which firm i's constant long-run unit cost is c_i. Then, if $P(Q)$ is the industry inverse demand function, q_i is firm i's output, and $\bar{q}_i = Q - q_i$ is the output of firm i's rivals, firm i's *economic* profit is given by:

$$(2) \qquad \pi_i = [P(q_i + \bar{q}_i) - c_i]q_i.$$

The first-order condition for maximizing π_i can be written as follows:

$$(3) \qquad (P - c_i) = - q_i P' (1 + \lambda_i) = \eta S_i (1 + \lambda_i)P,$$

where $S_i = q_i/Q$ is firm i's market share, $\eta = - P'Q/P$ is the reciprocal of the (absolute value of) the industry elasticity of demand, and $\lambda_i = d\bar{q}_i/dq_i$ is firm i's conjectural derivative.

Game theorists tend to become apoplectic at the sight of quantities like λ_i, since they do not appear in game-theoretic equilibria. I use conjectural derivatives here, as they are used in much recent industry-specific work (following Iwata (1974)), to summarize conduct that may in fact be an imperfectly collusive equilibrium of a complex game played by real oligopolists. Generally, higher values of conjectural derivatives describe less-intense rivalry: all else equal, the higher is λ_i, the lower is firm i's output and the larger is the gap between price and its marginal cost.

Continuing the development above, substitution of (3) into (2) yields:

$$(4) \qquad \pi_i = \eta(1 + \lambda_i) (Pq_i)S_i.$$

Firm i's *accounting* profit (neglecting accounting errors) will equal π_i plus ρk_i, where ρ is the relevant competitive rate of return and k_i is the value of firm i's equilibrium capital stock. Adding ρk_i to both sides of (4) and dividing by k_i, we obtain an expression for firm i's accounting rate of return on assets:

$$(5) \qquad r_i = \rho + [\eta(1 + \lambda_i)]v_i S_i,$$

where $v_i = Pq_i/k_i$ is the reciprocal of firm i's observed capital/output ratio. In this model, firms with lower costs tend as a consequence to have higher market shares and higher rates of return.

Finally, if $\lambda_i = \lambda$ and $v_i = v$ for all firms in the industry,[12] the industry's average accounting rate of return is given by an S_i-weighted average of the r_i:

$$(6) \qquad \bar{r} = \rho + [\eta(1 + \lambda)v]H,$$

where $H = \Sigma(S_i)^2$ is the Herfindahl–Hirschman measure of seller concentration. The greater are the differences among the c_i, the larger will be H in this framework; concentration is endogenous in long-run equilibria.

Equation (6) directly rationalizes Demsetz's (1973) assertions: even if the intensity of rivalry, measured here by λ, does not vary among industries, equation (6) predicts a positive correlation between concentration and profitability in cross-section. Random inter-industry differences in η and v could easily account for the general weakness of that correlation in practice. This view of the world cannot be distinguished from that of Bain in industry-level cross-sections. Many recent authors have accordingly turned to the analysis of intra-industry differences between firms, I discuss some of this work in section 5.

It is important to note that endogeneity problems of this sort are ubiquitous in cross-section studies in industrial organization. Such studies can at best detect differences among long-run equilibria. But essentially all observable quantities in any market are determined by what Scherer (1980: ch. 1) has called the market's *basic conditions* (particularly the nature of the product and the available technologies for production and marketing) and by business strategies, government policies, and historical accidents. Not only are basic conditions difficult to observe and quantify, but they too are endogenous in the long run as firms invest in product and process innovation.

This argument casts considerable doubt on the ability of cross-section studies in general to reveal structural relations. Consider, for instance, the strong positive cross-section relation between industry advertising-sales ratios and profitability first detected by Comanor and Wilson (1967) and subsequently found by numerous

---

[12] See Schmalensee 1987*a* for a discussion of more complex cases.

other authors. Even if this relation is not an accounting artifact, reflecting merely the failure to treat advertising with long-lived effects as an investment, it surely cannot be structural. If it were, it would imply that colluding firms could always increase their profits by increasing their advertising budgets, and this is most implausible. In this case, and in others, cross-section studies are best understood as revealing descriptive relations among endogenous variables. Such relations can be informative, but they must be interpreted with considerable care in light of the generally unobservable differences in exogenous variables that they reflect.

Finally, it is worth noting that there is some tension between the weak and inconclusive results of industry-level cross-section analyses and the fairly stark picture painted by many case studies. The latter show many apparent instances of non-competitive behaviour in concentrated industries; the former find relatively little evidence that concentrated industries earn monopoly profit. This suggests that profits are often eroded by forces other than rivalry among established firms. I discuss this suggestion further below.

4. Econometric Industry Studies

The discussion so far indicates that substantive progress in industrial organization depends critically on the productive use of non-classical approaches to empirical research. And a number of promising methods of this sort have been developed—some recently and some during the heyday of classical cross-section profitability studies. I begin here with promising approaches to the analysis of individual industries and then consider inter-industry analysis in section 5.

In recent years a number of authors have begun to heed Leonard Weiss's (1971: 398) call to go 'back to the industry study, but this time with regression in hand'. By focusing on a single industry, they can control for the unobservable differences in basic conditions that often plague the interpretation of cross-section studies. This focus of course also means that no single study can yield more than one observation on the industries that make up the economy. But many scholars have learned from the history of cross-section profitability regressions that it is better to understand one industry well than to collect difficult-to-interpret data on many.

By exploiting econometric techniques that were in large part unavailable to the authors of the classic industry studies discussed in section 2, scholars today can exploit more fully the information in available data. In some studies, which I discuss first, this information comes from differences among separated markets in the same industry; in others the useful variations occur over time in a single market.

Inter-Market Variation

An early exemplar of this line of research is Benham's (1972) study of the advertising of eyeglasses. Benham observed that some states in the United States made it illegal for eyeglass vendors to advertise, while others barred only advertising that mentioned prices, and still others had no restrictions at all. Benham gathered data on prices charged for eyeglasses in various states and found that the more severe were advertising restrictions, the higher were prices on average. This does not prove that advertising tends to increase rivalry in all settings, of course, though it does seem to indicate that it can do so under some conditions—most plausibly by reducing consumers' search costs.

A number of authors have reacted to the difficulty of measuring profitability and studied the relation between price and concentration in geographically separated markets, often with proxy variables for cost differences inserted as controls. Cotterill's (1986) study of supermarket pricing in Vermont towns provides a recent example. Most studies of this sort find seller concentration to be positively related to price. This work thus seems to provide relatively strong support for a link between concentration and collusion, since Demsetz's arguments would associate concentration with efficiency and thus with low prices. But the sources of spatial variations in concentration have not been systematically explored. And both trivial and substantial concentration effects have been detected, suggesting that the concentration-collusion relation, if any, has a substantial product-specific dimension.

In an interesting recent variation on this general theme, Bresnahan and Reiss (1987) study the number of retail establishments of various types (including veterinarians, beauticians, and cinemas) operating in a set of small, isolated towns in the United States. For each type of establishment they basically estimate two parameters:

P_1, the minimum population at which a single firm enters, and P_2, the minimum population at which a second firm appears. If (P_2/P_1) is approximately 2, entrants into one-firm markets must expect monopoly pricing to continue after their entry; values of (P_2/P_1) much above 2 indicate less favourable post-entry expectations and are thus consistent with entry deterrence. Bresnahan and Reiss find a good deal of variation in this ratio; they wisely resist the temptation to explore possible sources of inter-industry differences in their small sample.

Finally, Bresnahan (1987) uses quality differences to identify year-specific inter-market variation within the United States car industry. He employs a model of vertical product differentiation, which implies that small changes in the price of any one model of car affect only the two models with 'adjacent' quality levels. Because rivalry is thus localized along the quality spectrum, the overall car market can be decomposed into a set of linked submarkets. Estimated relations between pricing behaviour and the identities of the participants in each submarket can then be used to test hypotheses about firm behaviour. Bresnahan cannot reject collusive behaviour in 1954 and 1956; he cannot reject competitive behaviour for the boom year of 1955.

Intertemporal Variation

A number of studies have analysed changes in market behaviour following some arguably exogenous event, often related to government policy. Rose (1987), for instance, compares the United States trucking industry before and after deregulation and finds strong evidence that trade unions captured a large fraction of the rents created by regulatory restrictions on competition. Such rent-sharing seems plausible a priori, and many economists believe it accounts at least in part for the small inter-industry variations in profitability discussed in section 3. But it has proven hard to detect rent-sharing in inter-industry studies, in part because concentration and unionization are highly correlated in United States cross-sections.[13]

Mergers naturally lend themselves to 'before' and 'after' analyses of this sort, and a large literature on the effects of mergers has emerged in recent years. Barton and Sherman (1984), for instance, studied a merger that substantially increased concentration and

[13] But see Salinger 1984 for an interesting attempt and some striking results.

found that prices rose sharply after it was consummated. Many authors have found that acquired firms' shareholders generally benefit from mergers. Eckbo (1985) found that horizontal mergers also tend to benefit shareholders of rival firms. This finding might suggest that horizontal mergers tend to increase the likelihood of collusive behaviour, but Eckbo's finding that rival firms' stock-price increases were unrelated to the level of or change in seller concentration indicates that something more than a simple concentration-collusion relation is at work.

Many authors have recently used variations in behaviour over time in periods without clearly significant exogenous events to measure the extent to which monopoly power is being exercised.[14] Their studies are the most direct descendants of the classical industry studies discussed in section 2. This research involves a particularly heavy investment in data set construction and in developing modelling strategies tailored to available industry-specific data. Accordingly, a large number of techniques for econometric industry analysis have been developed, but most have been employed only once or twice.

Lieberman's (1987) analysis of capacity expansion decisions in chemical-process industries is an interesting, though somewhat atypical example of this general approach. Because of scale economies, new capacity in these industries is generally added in sizeable lumps, typically after a period of high utilization of existing capacity. Lieberman looks for significant differences between the decision rules used by established firms to add capacity and those used by new entrants, and he finds none. This finding casts doubt on the empirical validity of the many models in which over-investment in capacity is used to deter entry. Slade's (1987) use of daily petrol station price data (along with daily data on the wholesale price of petrol) to estimate reaction functions provides another recent example of the direct estimation of firm decision rules.

Many recent econometric industry studies rely on variants of the static first-order condition written above as equation (3):

$$(7) \qquad P_i = MC_i + [(1 + \lambda_i)P'_i]q_i$$

where MC_i replaces c_i to emphasize that marginal cost is what

[14] See Bresnahan 1988 for a comprehensive and useful survey of this work.

matters, and P_i replaces P because different firms may charge different prices when products are differentiated. If sufficient time-series data on cost and demand conditions are available, one can use this relation to estimate or test hypotheses about the intensity of rivalry, measured here by λ_i.

In an influential early paper, Iwata (1974) studied a homogeneous-product industry and used estimates of the industry demand function and accounting estimates of firm-specific marginal costs to estimate conjectural derivatives. Most subsequent authors have avoided accounting estimates of marginal cost and have instead used data on its determinants. These usually include input prices and capacity utilization, though Ashenfelter and Sullivan (1987) employ data on changes in state-specific cigarette taxes to construct (non-parametric) tests on λ.

Baker and Bresnahan (1985) observe in effect that (7) implies that a firm with market power will price according to

$$(8) \qquad (P_i - MC_i)/P_i = - (1 + \lambda_i)P_i'q_i/P_i = 1/\epsilon_i^r,$$

where the last equality defines ϵ_i^r, firm i's net or residual elasticity of demand. This quantity measures the sensitivity of firm i's demand to changes in its price, taking into account the expected responses of i's rivals. Assuming expectations are on average correct, Baker and Bresnahan show how to use data on demand and on firm-specific determinants of marginal cost to obtain estimates of firm-specific residual demand elasticities—and thus of mark-ups over marginal cost.

As Bresnahan (1988) notes, econometric industry studies generally reject competitive hypotheses in favour of alternatives involving less intense rivalry. Like the classical industry studies discussed in section 2, this work often relies on data made public in antitrust proceedings. It is thus perhaps no great surprise that non-competitive behaviour is frequently detected. And, as I noted in section 3, profit rates do not appear to be extraordinarily high in many industries in which price is found to be well above marginal cost. Thus, the results of econometric industry studies do not serve to rule out Chamberlinian monopolistic competition or other models in which entry or inflated fixed costs eliminates potential monopoly profits.

Recent work by Hall (1987) illustrates both the potential value of time-series data in industrial organization and a potential pitfall in their analysis. Suppose that capital is fixed in the short run and that a firm's production function is simply $Q = vL$, where v is a constant and L is labour input.[15] If w is the wage rate, it follows that short-run marginal cost is equal to w/v. Suppose that the firm sets price, P, equal to θ times marginal cost, where θ is a constant. Taking first differences in the production function then yields:

$$(9)\ \frac{\Delta Q}{Q} - \frac{\Delta L}{L} = \left[\frac{vL}{Q} - 1\right]\frac{\Delta L}{L} = \left[\theta\frac{wL}{PQ} - 1\right]\frac{\Delta L}{L},$$

where the last expression follows because $P = \theta w/v$. Since all quantities in (9) except θ are observable, simple time-series regressions can be used to estimate θ. And, since labour productivity is observed to vary pro-cyclically (Q/L rises when L rises and falls when it falls) and labour's share of revenue (wL/PQ) is less than one, Hall's estimates of θ are generally well above unity for two-digit United States industries.

Hall's analysis rests on a static model of firm conduct. In fact, as Carlton (1986) and others have noted, prices tend to be rigid over time, particularly in concentrated industries. Rotemberg and Summers (1988) argue that price rigidity and the related practice of labour hoarding (work-force rigidity) can produce pro-cyclical variations in labour productivity in competitive industries. It would seem that dynamic models of the firm should be used to analyse changes in business behaviour over time; the traditional cross-section assumption of long-run equilibrium may be highly misleading in a time-series context.

5.   Inter-Industry Studies

Even though cross-section industry-level profitability studies are still out of fashion, studies comparing multiple industries appear regularly in leading journals. Only this sort of research can directly reveal patterns that hold for the economy as a whole. A hallmark of recent inter-industry research is the development of data sets that

---

[15] Hall (1987) in fact works with a general neoclassical production function with multiple inputs, but his analysis is quite similar to that which follows.

contain information not present in the industry-level cross-sections on which the bulk of the earlier literature was based. As in section 4, the discussion here is organized around the sources of that information.

International Differences

Comparisons between the same industry in countries at a similar stage in development hold basic conditions of products and available technologies at least approximately constant.[16] The best-known example of this sort of study may still be Pryor's (1972) comparison of concentration ratios in manufacturing industries. Pryor found that rank correlations of these ratios among industrialized nations were high, suggesting the importance of basic conditions—as opposed to business strategies, government policies, and historical accidents—as determinants of concentration. Moreover, he found that concentration did not tend to decline noticeably with the size of the national market except for very small nations; for one reason or another, larger countries tend to have larger firms. (See Scherer, *et al.* (1975) for more on this.)

Several Canadian and United States scholars have taken advantage of language and geography and studied correlates of differences between Canadian manufacturing industries and their United States counterparts. The comprehensive study by Caves, Porter, and Spence (1980) is an important example of this strand of research.

Survey and Interview Data

Perhaps because economists tend to compare themselves with natural scientists, particularly physicists, most economic research in recent years has been based entirely on data about what firms and households actually *do* in the market, rather than on direct measures of attitudes, information, and beliefs. Most econometric industry studies, for instance, eschew reliance on the qualitative documentary information and testimony that were key data for the authors of the classic industry studies.

To some extent this practice reflects a belief, not present in the other social and behavioural sciences, that one can learn about people only by observing their actions, not by asking them

[16] See Caves 1988 for a comprehensive and stimulating survey of research of this general sort.

questions. The result is that no information at all is obtained regarding the likely outcomes of experiments that nature does not perform, and variables that are not captured by conventional accounting systems or directly reflected in securities prices are not measured. Moreover, the difficulty of obtaining comparable numerical data over long periods tends to discourage work on the evolution of market structure on conduct, themes that were central to the classic case studies.

Some very interesting inter-industry work has been produced by setting these prejudices aside. There is a long tradition of 'engineering' studies of scale economies, which are essentially based on structured interview; Scherer, *et al.* (1975) is a leading example. This research aims to map out the features of best-practice technology directly, rather than trying to infer it from numerical data on plants of various (typically unknown) vintages and scales.

Porter's (1976) work on the influence of retailer behaviour on market performance gives an example of the potential value of judgemental classifications of industries—in the tradition of Bain (1956) Porter made use of common sense and information about distribution channels to divide consumer products into 'shopping goods', for which retailers are an important source of information, and 'convenience goods', which retailers simply make available. Estimation of standard cross-section profitability equations produced very different results in these two samples, suggesting, consistent with recent theory, that information transmission mechanisms are important for market performance.

Most recently, Levin, *et al.* (1987) conducted a large survey study aimed at detecting, among other things, what factors prevent rapid imitation from dissipating the rewards to innovation. Their findings that patents are unimportant in this regard in many industries and that the important factors vary considerably from industry to industry have a number of implications for theoretical and empirical research on technical change.

Intra-Industry Differences

As section 3 noted, Demsetz's (1973) critique of the classical interpretation of cross-section profitability regressions focused attention on differences among rival firms. The first studies of these differences seemed strongly to favour Demsetz's position. Porter

(1979) found (as had Bain (1951)) that the profitability of leading firms was positively correlated with concentration, but the profitability of firms with small market shares was not.[17] Ravenscraft (1983) included both concentration and market share in equations designed to explain business unit profitability. He and a number of later authors found that the coefficient of market share was positive and significant in such regressions, while the coefficient of concentration was not.

Later studies that looked more closely at the inter-industry pattern of intra-industry differences produced less clear-cut results. A number of authors found that the intra-industry relation between profitability and market share on which Demsetz's argument seemed to rest was not particularly strong in many cases. Schmalensee (1987*a*) estimated equation (5) for a matched sample of United States manufacturing industries in 1963 and 1972 and replicated this finding. He then studied the inter-industry differences in the estimated coefficients and found little support for simple models of either the Bain or Demsetz variety. He did detect, as had several other authors, a positive cross-section relation between the coefficient of market share in (5) and the industry advertising-sales ratio. A possible explanation for these mixed results is that both Bain and Demsetz are right, but the relative importance of the mechanisms they stress varies considerably across the economy.

A number of studies support the importance of further research at the firm and business unit levels. Schmalensee (1985) found that the intra-industry variation in business unit profit rates considerably exceeds the inter-industry variation and that knowledge of a firm's profitability in one of its lines of business does not in general help predict how well its other businesses will do. Later work by Mueller (1986) and Cubbin and Geroski (1987) suggests that the performance of individual firms, particularly market leaders, over time tends to be at most weakly related to average performance of the markets in which they operate. Mueller finds that market shares of leading firms are surprisingly stable over time in many industries. All of this says that Demsetz was clearly right in one important

[17] Porter (1979) argued that his results did not imply that Demsetz was right but were rather more consistent with the existence of important strategic groups within industries and with mobility barriers that prevented movement into the more profitable groups.

respect: industry averages generally hide a great deal of interesting intra-industry variation.

Intertemporal Differences

If a cross-section of industries is observed over time, changes in the pattern of inter-industry relations may provide valuable information. Some recent studies have employed this sort of panel data, though little use has yet been made of the sophisticated econometric techniques that have been developed for the analysis of such data.

In a study concerned with the Demsetz (1973) critique, Peltzman (1977) examined the relation between changes in concentration and changes in price and productivity. He found that concentration increases tended to be associated with above-average increases in both price-cost margins and productivity and (because the productivity effect was stronger) below-average increases in prices. Later work by Gisser (1984) and others finds that productivity gains are associated with both substantial increases *and* substantial decreases in concentration. These results suggest a generalized version of Demsetz's world view: innovators gain at the expense of their rivals, so that concentration is endogenous in the long run, but concentration may rise or fall depending on whether initially large or small firms are the innovators.

Domowitz, Hubbard, and Petersen (1986) have constructed an industry-level panel data set for United States manufacturing that covers the 1958-81 period. Their research reveals, among other things, that the concentration-profitability correlation fell dramatically in the 1970s and that it moved pro-cyclically around this trend. In related work, Schmalensee (1987*b*) found that the average intra-industry profitability advantage of large firms over their smaller rivals also declined over this period but that the large-firm advantage moved counter-cyclically.

To interpret these results, it is useful to rewrite equations (5) and (6) in somewhat more general form:

$$(5') \qquad r_i = \rho + \delta S_i \qquad \text{(firm level)},$$

$$(6') \qquad \bar{r} = \rho + \delta H \qquad \text{(industry level)}.$$

Schmalensee finds in effect that δ on average declines over time.

Equation (6') indicates that this can explain (in a mechanical sense) the secular decline in the correlation between concentration and profitability reported by Domowitz, Hubbard, and Petersen. But Schmalensee also finds that δ on average moves counter-cyclically in (5'), while Domowitz, Hubbard, and Petersen find the correlation between concentration and profitability to be pro-cyclical. This suggests that ρ, which is best interpreted here as the profit rate earned by small firms, is more strongly pro-cyclical in concentrated than in unconcentrated industries. This in turn suggests that the incidence of collusive behaviour in concentrated industries, which can be expected to raise the profits of both small and large firms, may be pro-cyclical.

Finally, Dunne, Roberts, and Samuelson (1987) use a panel data set constructed by linking information gathered by the United States Census of Manufacturing at five-year intervals at the plant and firm levels. They are thus able to study a relatively complete record of entry and exit in United States manufacturing industries over time and to distinguish among entry by new firms, firms that build new plants, and firms that change the product mix of existing plants. Among their more interesting findings are that both entry and exit are frequent events in most United States industries and that entry rates and exit rates are positively correlated in cross-section. It is hard to come away from their study with the impression that entry-deterring behaviour is important in many United States manufacturing industries.

6.   Conclusions and Implications

Until game-theoretic analysis either begins to yield robust, un-ambiguous predictions or is replaced by a mode of theorizing that does so, any major substantive advances in industrial organization are likely to come from empirical research. And the recent increase in the volume of high-quality empirical studies makes it quite possible that industrial organization will once again become a field driven by facts rather than theories.

The examples discussed in sections 4 and 5 indicate that well-designed empirical research can reveal a good deal about how market structure, conduct, and performance are shaped. But knowledge of many phenomena is clearly still thin in important respects. One of the few substantive conclusions that can be confidently asserted at this stage is that while market concentration may indeed have some impact on conduct and performance, it is much less important than Bain and some of his early followers seem to have believed. It seems unlikely that any very simple model of business behaviour will prove empirically robust.

It is important to note that virtually all of the persuasive empirical studies discussed here share one important feature: they employ carefully constructed data sets. Because few real data sets confess their secrets easily, advances in modelling techniques and econometric methods are important. But the main lesson that seems to emerge from recent developments in empirical research in industrial organization is that the quality of the results obtained depends critically on the quality of the data employed. The key dimension of quality has more to do with experimental design than with measurement error; what matters most is whether the data contain information that can be used to identify the answers to questions of economic interest.

This is in some respects a discouraging conclusion. Economists, unlike historians or anthropologists, are formally trained only in the analysis of data sets, not in their construction. The economics profession does not much reward the tedious labour necessary to construct sound and interesting data sets. And data-set construction is particularly difficult in industrial organization, and not only because accounting data are imperfect. Large modern firms are complex collections of business units operating in different markets, each with a whole array of tangible and intangible assets and employing a large number of workers and managers, linked by top executives and their staffs. Business firms typically produce large quantities of data to guide their own decisions, but they are almost universally reluctant to make much of this information public. The labour economist's task of describing workers and their behaviour seems to pale beside the difficulties inherent in constructing data sets on firms and their decisions and operations.

The economics profession seems unlikely dramatically to change its collective attitude towards data collection in the foreseeable future. Thus, progress in industrial organization may depend critically on the extent to which the construction of informative data sets is supported by government agencies and other sources of research financing.

References

Alberts, W. W. (1984), 'Do Oligopolists Earn "Noncompetitive" Rates of Return?' *American Economic Review*, 74: 624–32.

Ashenfelter, O. and Sullivan, D. (1987), 'Nonparametric Tests of Market Structure: An Application to the Cigarette Industry', *Journal of Industrial Economics*, 35: 483–98.

Bain, J. S. (1951), 'Relation of Profit Rate to Industry Concentration: American Manufacturing, 1936–1940', *Quarterly Journal of Economics*, 65: 293–324.

—— (1956), *Barriers to New Competition*, Harvard University Press, Cambridge, Mass.

Baker, J. B. and Bresnahan, T. F. (1985), 'The Gains from Merger or Collusion in Product-Differentiated Industries', *Journal of Industrial Economics*, 33: 427–44.

Barton, D. M. and Sherman, R. (1984) 'The Price and Profit Effects of Horizontal Merger: A Case Study', *Journal of Industrial Economics*, 33: 165–77.

Benham, L. (1972), 'The Effects of Advertising on the Price of Eyeglasses', *Journal of Law and Economics*, 15: 337–52.

Bresnahan, T. F. (1987), 'Competition and Collusion in the American Automobile Industry: The 1955 Price War', *Journal of Industrial Economics*, 35: 457–82.

—— (1988), 'Empirical Studies of Industries with Market Power', in R. Schmalensee and R. D. Willig (eds.), *Handbook of Industrial Organization*, North-Holland, Amsterdam.

—— and Reiss, P. C. (1987), 'What Kinds of Markets Have Too Few Firms?' mimeo., Standford University Working Paper.

—— and Schmalensee, R, (1987), 'The Empirical Renaissance in Industrial Economics: An Overview', *Journal of Industrial Economics*, 35: 371–8.

Carlton, D. W. (1986), 'The Rigidity of Prices', *American Economic Review*, 76: 637–58.

Caves, R. E. (1988), 'International Differences in Industrial Organization', in R. Schmalensee and R. D. Willig (eds.), *Handbook of Industrial Organization*, North-Holland, Amsterdam.

—— Porter, M. E., and Spence, A. M. (1980), *Competition in the Open Economy: A Model Applied to Canada*, Harvard University Press, Cambridge, Mass.

Clapham, J. H. (1922), 'Of Empty Economic Boxes', *Economic Journal*, 32: 305–14.

Clarke, R., Davies, S. W., and Waterson, M. (1984), 'The Profitability–Concentration Relation: Market Power or Efficiency?', *Journal of Industrial Economics*, 32: 435–50.

Comanor, W. S. and Wilson, T. A. (1967), 'Advertising, Market Structure and Performance', *Review of Economics and Statistics*, 49: 423–40.

Cotterill, R. S. (1986), 'Market Power in the Retail Food Industry: Evidence from Vermont', *Review of Economics and Statistics*, 68: 379–86.

Cowling, K. and Waterson, M. (1976), 'Price–Cost Margins and Market Structure', *Economica*, 43: 267–74.

Cox, R. (1933), *Competition in the American Tobacco Industry*, Columbia University Press, New York.

Cubbin, J. and Geroski, P. A. (1987), 'The Convergence of Profits in the Long Run: Inter-firm and Inter-industry Comparisons', *Journal of Industrial Economics*, 35: 427–42.

Demsetz, H. (1973), 'Industry Structure, Market Rivalry, and Public Policy', *Journal of Law and Economics*, 16: 1–10.

Domowitz, I., Hubbard, R. G. and Petersen, B. G. (1986), 'Business Cycles and the Relationship between Concentration and Price-Cost Margins', *Rand Journal of Economics*, 17: 1–17.

Dunne, T., Roberts, M. J., and Samuelson, L. (1987), 'Patterns of Firm Entry and Exit in U.S. Manufacturing Industries', mimeo., Pennsylvania State University.

Eckbo, B. E. (1985), 'Mergers and the Market Concentration Doctrine: Evidence from the Capital Market', *Journal of Business*, 58: 325–49.

Fisher, F. M. and McGowan, J. J. (1983), 'On the Misuse of Accounting Rates of Return to Infer Monopoly Profits', *American Economic Review*, 73: 82–97.

Friedman, M. (1953), 'The Methodology of Positive Economics', in id., *Essays in Positive Economics*, University of Chicago Press, Chicago, Ill.

Fudenberg, D. and Tirole, J. (1987), 'Understanding Rent Dissipation: On the Use of Game Theory in Industrial Organization', *American Economic Review, Papers and Proceedings*, 77: 176–83.

Gisser, M. (1984), 'Price Leadership and Dynamic Aspects of Oligopoly in U.S. Manufacturing', *Journal of Political Economy*, 92: 1035–48.

Goldschmid, H. J., Mann, H. Michael, and Weston, J. Fred (eds.) (1974), *Industrial Concentration: The New Learning*, Little Brown, Boston, Mass.

Hall, R. E. (1987), 'The Relation between Price and Marginal Cost in U.S. Industry', mimeo., Hoover Institution, Stanford University.

Harberger, A. C. (1954), 'Monopoly and Resource Allocation', *American Economic Review, Papers and Proceedings*, 44: 77–87.

Iwata, G. (1974), 'Measurement of Conjectural Variations in Oligopoly', *Econometrica*, 42: 947–66.

Levin, R. C., Klevorick, A. K., Nelson, R. R., and Winter, S. G. (1987), 'Appropriating the Returns from Industrial R & D', mimeo., Yale University.

Lieberman, M. H. (1987), 'Excess Capacity as a Barrier to Entry: An Empirical Appraisal', *Journal of Industrial Economics*, 35: 607–27.

Liebowitz, S. J. (1982), 'What do Census Price-Cost Margins Measure?' *Journal of Law and Economics*, 25: 231–46.

Milgrom, P. and Roberts, J. (1987), 'Informational Asymmetries, Strategic Behaviour, and Industrial Organization', *American Economic Review, Papers and Proceedings*, 77: 184–93.

Mueller, D. C. (1986), *Profits in the Long Run*, Cambridge University Press, Cambridge.

Nicholls, W. H. (1951), *Price Policies in the Cigarette Industry*, Vanderbilt University Press, Nashville, Tennessee.

Peck, M. J. (1961), *Competition in the Aluminum Industry: 1945–1958*, Harvard University Press, Cambridge, Mass.

Peltzman, S. (1977), 'The Gains and Losses from Industrial Concentration', *Journal of Law and Economics*, 20: 229–64.

Plott, C. R. (1988), 'An Updated Review of Industrial Organization Applications of Experimental Methods', in R. Schmalensee and R. D. Willig (eds.), *Handbook of Industrial Organization*, North-Holland, Amsterdam.

Porter, M. E. (1976), *Interbrand Choice, Strategy, and Bilateral Market Power*, Harvard University Press, Cambridge, Mass.

—— (1979), 'The Structure Within Industries and Companies' Performance', *Review of Economics and Statistics*, 61: 214–27.

Pryor, F. L. (1972), 'An International Comparison of Concentration Ratios', *Review of Economics and Statistics*, 54: 130–40.

Ravenscraft, D. J. (1983), 'Structure-Profit Relationships at the Line of Business and Industry Level', *Review of Economics and Statistics*, 65: 22–31.

Rose, N. L. (1987), 'Labor Rent-Sharing and Regulation: Evidence from the Trucking Industry', *Journal of Political Economy*, 95: 1146–78.

Rotemberg, J. and Summers L. E. (1988), 'Labor Hoarding, Inflexible Prices, and Procyclical Productivity', mimeo, MIT.

Salinger, M. (1984), 'Tobin's q, Unionization, and the Concentration-Profits Relationship', *Rand Journal of Economics*, 15: 159–70.

Scherer, F. M. (1980), *Industrial Market Structure and Economic Performance*, 2nd edn., Rand-McNally, Chicago, Ill.

—— Beckstein, A., Kaufer, E., and Murphy, R. D. (1975), *The Economics of Multi-Plant Operation*, Harvard University Press, Cambridge, Mass.

Schmalensee, R. (1972), *The Economics of Advertising*, North-Holland, Amsterdam.

—— (1985), 'Do Markets Differ Much?' *American Economic Review*, 75: 341–51.

—— (1987*a*), 'Collusion versus Differential Efficiency: Testing Alternative Hypotheses', *Journal of Industrial Economics*, 35: 399–425.

—— (1987*b*), 'Intra-Industry Profitability Differences in U.S. Manufacturing', 1953–1983', mimeo., MIT.

—— (1988), 'Inter-Industry Studies of Structure and Performance', in id. and R. D. Willig (eds.), *Handbook of Industrial Organization*, North-Holland, Amsterdam.

Slade, M. E. (1987), 'Interfirm Rivalry in a Repeated Game: An Empirical Test of Tacit Collusion', *Journal of Industrial Economics*, 35: 499–516.

Tennant, R. B. (1950), *The American Cigarette Industry*, Yale University Press, New Haven, Conn.

Tirole, J. (1988), *The Theory of Industrial Organization*, MIT Press, Cambridge, Mass.

Wallace, D. H. (1937), *Market Control in the Aluminum Industry*, Harvard University Press, Cambridge, Mass.

Weiss, L. W. (1971), 'Quantitative Studies of Industrial Organization', in M. D. Intriligator (ed.), *Frontiers of Quantitative Economics*, North-Holland, Amsterdam.

Index